KENT LARSON WITH PAT HAHN, JASON BISHOP AND MAX McALLISTER

MOTORBOOKS

MOTORCYCLE
TRACK DAY
HANDBOOK

First published in 2004 by Motorbooks, an imprint of MBI Publishing Company, Galtier Plaza, Suite 200, 380 Jackson Street, St. Paul, MN 55101-3885 USA

Motorbooks titles are also available at discounts in bulk quantity for industrial or sales-promotional use. For details write to Special Sales Manager at MBI Publishing Company, Galtier Plaza, Suite 200, 380 Jackson Street, St. Paul, MN 55101-3885 USA.

Library of Congress Cataloging-in-Publication Data
Larson, Kent, 1964-
   Motorcycle track day handbook/ by Kent Larson, Pat Hahn,
     and Jason Bishop
   p. cm.
   ISBN 0-7603-1761-5 (alk. paper)
   1. Motorcycle track days--Handbooks, manuals, etc.
   I. Hahn, Pat, 1969-II. Bishop, Jason. III. Title

GV1060.155.L37 2005
796.7'5--dc22

Editorial: Darwin Holmstrom
Design: Brenda Canales

Printed in China

Cover photo courtesy Lee Parks
Frontispiece photo courtesy Jack Beaudry
Title page photo courtesy Brian J. Nelson
Back cover photo courtesy Tony Marx

CONTENTS

ACKNOWLEDGMENTS

I sit in front of a computer screen showing a blank document awaiting input. My current task—writing these acknowledgments—waits as my mind's eye travels back in time to the same screen two years ago. The slightly younger, and far less wise, copy of me is staring at a blank document wondering how to put together the thoughts and words needed to complete his first book.

Floating up and down the time stream—sampling memories of events, conversations, and emotions—reveals the greatest misconception I had as I started the task: I thought I was going to have to do it alone. I now know that completing this book by myself was not only unnecessary but also impossible. I have many to thank for the product you now hold in your hands.

I'll start by thanking my good friends and fellow contributors to this book: Darwin Holmstrom, Pat Hahn, Jason Bishop, and Max McAllister. Without their help this book wouldn't be as good and probably wouldn't have been completed.

Darwin is my editor, motivator, and instigator. He conceived the project, kept us on task, and polished the output. I pray he is as happy with the result as I.

Pat and Jason are riding buddies and accomplished wordsmiths. You'll find insights from Jason as he describes his first track experience in Chapter Three and the step up to club racing in Chapter Six. Pat Hahn is the best-selling author of *Ride Hard, Ride Smart* and helped me here with most of Chapter Seven. Pat also greatly contributed to Chapter Five and was always there as a sounding board for my ideas. Thanks guys!

Max McAllister is the president of Traxxion Dynamics and my go-to guy for suspension issues. With Max's contribution, Chapter Four has come together as one of the best introductions to motorcycle suspension setup I've seen anywhere. Thanks, Max, for pulling together this great tool for getting your bike dialed.

Darwin Holmstrom, Peter Schletty, and Brenda Canales deserve special mention for making the book look so good. I know they are "just doing their jobs" as acquisitions editor, associate editor, and book designer for MBI Publishing, but I greatly appreciate them doing their jobs so well.

Many friends provided photographs for nothing more than simple recognition of their work. Their names can be found after the captions. Their contribution is greatly appreciated. The pros delivered beautiful shots of far greater value than the small fees charged. I highly recommend the following professional photographers: Jack Beaudry of Slider Photo (www.sliderphoto.com), Jonah Klevesahl of Momentum Photo (www.momentumphoto.net), Brian J. Nelson (www.brianjnelson.com), and Tom Starbuck of Starbuck Photography.

My personal thanks goes to the general motorcycle community. From John Altman, Steve Morici, and later Steve Guitoli (the dorks who taught me to ride), to Craig Nekola, Paul Ellman, Fred Dunken, and Brian Lacy (the CRA and CCS racers who taught me how to ride faster), and all the members from the CBR list, MN-Sportbike list, and NESBA discussion board (large communities of interesting riders). Motorcycle people are the best people in the world. I'm proud to be part of these extended families. Thanks to Lee Parks for letting me contribute a chapter to his best selling book *Total Control*. That was the opportunity which morphed into the chance to write this book.

I want to thank God for my family. My wonderful wife, Susan, and the two beautiful miracles we were given in Lizabeth and Duke. They bring me almost as much joy as motorcycles. Well, OK, they bring me the most joy. For them, I would give up bikes. Because of their love and support, I don't have to make that sacrifice. I am truly blessed.

Moving on to professional thanks, I want to call out the companies and individuals who have provided top notch products and services over the years. These companies have provided support during my racing and writing careers. Their support has spanned the range from free

to full-priced, but be assured no one made this list by buying their way in. Free crap is still crap. I only list companies here who I strongly recommend as the best source for a given product.

The companies below are my personal recommendations as sources for good products, great service, and top value. If you need something, consider these companies first. If they don't live up to your expectations, let me know (kent@larsonroadracing.com) so I can help remedy the issue or take them off my best-of list.

Favorite tuner:
Hitman Motorsports
www.hitmanmotorsports.com
4120 Hoffman Road
White Bear Lake, MN 55110
(651) 762-8031

Beautiful racing engine covers, sure-shift kits, jet kits, and various go-fast parts:
Factory Pro Tuning
www.factorypro.com
179 Paul Drive
San Rafael, CA 94903
Orders: (800) 869-0497
Tech Support: (415) 491-5920
Shop Work: (415) 472-4962

Go-fast bits for Aprilias:
AF1 Racing
www.af1racing.com
918 Banyon St.
Austin, TX 78757
(512) 459-DYNO (3966)

Suspension components and consulting:
Traxxion Dynamics
www.traxxion.com
(770) 592-3823

Race Tech
www.racetech.com
(951) 279-6655

Brake pads and rotors:
FERODO
www.ferodousa.com
4200 Diplomacy Road
Fort Worth, TX 76155
Toll Free: (866) ferodo1
Tech Support: info@ferodousa.com

Sprockets, chains, clip-ons, and rear-sets:
Vortex Racing
www.vortexracing.com
Odessa, FL
(800) 440-3559

Clip-ons, rear-sets, frame sliders, and ceramic hybrid bearings:
Woodcraft
info@woodcraft-cfm.com
www.woodcraft-cfm.com
Mansfield, MA
(508) 339-5772

Parts and accessories with great service and good prices:
Knee Draggers
www.kneedraggers.com
(877) 294-2920

Zanotti Motor Company
zanmot@aol.com
www.zanottimotor.com
170 Pittsburg Road
Butler, PA 16001
(724) 283-2777

Bodywork:
Armour Bodies
info@armourbodies.ca
www.armourbodies.com
North Bay, Ontario
North America Toll Free: (877) 944-8244

Used parts:
You can always dig around on eBay and find some good deals, but that requires more patience than I usually have. I'd rather see a good online classified advertisement where I can accept or make an offer right now, without waiting for an auction to end. Here are some recommended sources for classified ads:
www.superbikeplanet.com
www.2wf.com
http://forums.13x.com
www.cra-mn.com
All are good for finding things like a full set of mint street bodywork, specific good bits off crashed bikes, used racing parts,or even fully prepped race bikes from last season. In my experience, these sites all have a higher than normal "good guy to scammer" ratio, but as with any financial transaction, use care and common sense to avoid being ripped off.

Motorcycle stands:
Pit Bull Products, inc.
www.pit-bull.com
614 Pearl Avenue
Huntsville, AL 35801
(877) 533-1977

Dunlop tires and trackside service:
Midwest Roadrace
sales@midwestroadrace.com
(612) 369-0736

Michelin tires and setup advice:
Mason Racin' Tires
thetireguy2@msn.com
www.michelin.com/moto

Pirelli tires and setup advice:
Matt Drucker
MD Racing
matt@mdracingstp.com
www.mdracingstp.com
(309) 526-3246
Matt is the tuning, setup, and tire support services for all the Midwest www.nesba.com track days.

Ice-racing tires:
Heath Holste
wheelieheath@yahoo.com
(612) 290-1400
Heath will create the right tires for getting your dirt bike on the ice over winter. He knows the brands to use and how to lay out the screws for best grip. But call him early to get in the queue. Both the available tires and his available time run out quickly.

Helmets:
Shoei Safety Helmet Corporation
www.shoei-helmets.com to locate a dealer near you

Leathers, gloves, and boots:
www.newenough.com has great savings on used and close-out items as well as the best service around.

Leather repair and customization:
Tom the Tailor
www.zip-r-strip.com
1052 19th Avenue SE
Minneapolis, MN 55414
(612) 379-1723
(800) 379-2201

Knee pucks:
Jeff Lee
Asphalt & Gas
angjlee@yahoo.com
1041 Ardmore Ave.
Oakland, CA 94610
(510) 451-3044

Cool motorcycle racing related clothing:
Ignition Motorsports, Inc.
www.ignitionmoto.com or ask for it at your local motor-sports retailer.

Boots:
Helimot
helimot@aol.com
www.helimot.com
1141 Old Bayshore Hwy
San Jose CA 95112-2808
Phone: (408) 298-9608
Fax: (408) 271-3955
Helimot is the US distributor and a retail sales center for the Frey-Daytona brand of boots. The Frey-Daytona Security boot is the best protection for feet and ankles that I've ever found. They are also among the most expensive boots around but I could have avoided months of rehab had I only invested in them earlier.

Gloves and Total Control Advanced Riding Clinics:
Lee Parks Design
www.leeparksdesign.com
(800) 943-5638
Lee's deerskin and elkskin gloves are the strongest and most comfortable around. My editor crashed in Brainerd's infamous Turn One and Lee's deerskin gloves were the only piece of gear to survive the crash. Lee's Total Control Advanced Riding Clinics are the easiest way to improve your track-day skills in a controlled environment.

INTRODUCTION

I'm on my wife's R6 chasing a 748 down a twisty Wisconsin back road with a 929, Superhawk, SV650, and a couple of GSXRs stacked up behind me. We come to a blind right hander that wraps around a sheer cliff and the 748 zips out of sight around the bend. I go in wide to get a view of the surface and flick it over with the start of the curve looking clean; unfortunately, it was just the start that was clean.

Sometimes it would be nice if the real world included an <UNDO> command. The harder you ride, the greater the risk of a tumble. Would you rather have a deep gravel trap or a guard rail waiting to catch you? Jack Beaudry

half second later I see a 2-foot-wide patch of sand that was washed off the cliff. The patch was solid (no common car tire gaps) and spanned the road shoulder to shoulder. The 748 flopping around in the outside ditch also catches my attention. My brain says "Sand!" and my body stands the bike up and tosses it back down after the wheels are on the other side of the wash. I finish the corner and pull to the side. As I park the bike, I hear the horrible sound of metal and plastic being ground down by asphalt as the next bike in line piles in behind the 748.

Bike number 4 is able to stop just short of the bikes in the ditch with its front tire plowing into the sand on the outside of the turn. The rear wheel draws a groove through the mid-corner sand and a black line across the oncoming lane. By the time bike number 5 gets to the corner, the 748 rider has run back up the road and is flagging down people so things are a lot less dramatic. Everyone else just slows down and safely pulls over.

A few months later, I'm riding two up on a different section of the twisted Wisconsin secondary roads. It's a new road to me and I'm the lead rider of a pack of about 20 bikes. Everyone was warned that we'd be running a calm taking-my-wife-to-lunch pace but there's something about a group of bikes up your butt that brings out some extra aggression. I find myself pushing a little harder as the day goes on, trying to balance the desire for a large safety margin against the want to keep my followers from being bored.

We top a slight rise and the road disappears. It's just gone! There's nothing but grass and forest where I was expecting pavement. I'm hard on the brakes without a clue about which way to turn. My entire focus is pulled straight ahead at the rapidly approaching end of asphalt. I remember to modulate the back brake a few times as the rear wheel locks up and starts to step out sideways. The rest of my attention is focused on keeping the front wheel

Aftermath of the 748-initiated pileup. Dave Boucher

Start of the barbed-wire ride. Kent Larson

rolling but slowing as fast as possible. I see I'm not going to stop before the pavement ends.

At the last second I let go of the brakes and bounce into the field looking for a gap in the trees. There! No problem. It will be a rough ride across lumpy ground but I'm calming down because I see a peaceful end to my screw up. I continue to slow while steering into the gap that will take me through the grove and into an open field with plenty of room to stop. I am just starting to think about all the crap I am going to take from my fellow riders over lunch when I get the last-second revelation that the field is protected by a barbed-wire fence.

Thank God I had things slowed to the point that I was just pulled off the bike by the wire across my neck instead of having my head separated from my body. Thanks also that my body being pulled off caused the wire to go up and over my wife, Susan.

A few days later, I came back to look over this corner to find out where the road went. I make no excuses for being a dumb ass but I can see what happened. The road has a slight rise so you don't get to see where it goes until you come up the hill far enough. As you start up the hill, there are no signs to indicate a turn is coming, but you can see a signpost poking just into view directly in front of you. I remember seeing the signpost and thinking the road must jog slightly to the right to pass in front of the post. That let me switch from off throttle, waiting to see where the road was, to back on throttle with a little right-turn bias as I crested the hill.

Stopping at the top of the hill, you can see a hard left-turn arrow and the road making a sharp 90-degree turn to pass to the left of the sign post instead of on the expected right. Oops.

I bring up these two street incidents to point out the main benefit of getting to a racetrack. On a racetrack, you know what the corner is doing and what the pavement is like. You get to see the same corner every minute or so and can work up your speed slowly and comfortably. You don't just get a similar corner every so often like you do when street riding; you get the *exact same* corner.

At the track you don't get surprised by a sand wash or by the road going a different direction than you anticipate. You can free your attention from things such as traffic and road conditions to focus solely on what you are doing to control your bike.

Many experienced street riders get to the point where they don't have to think about what they do to control their bike.

They can brake, swerve, and accelerate to avoid the left-turning moron trying to kill them without thinking "the brake is the right lever." This allows time to think evil thoughts about the blind idiot's bloodline and still find the horn button or display the bird. (Have you ever noticed that on a bike you can't flip someone off and hit the horn at the same time?)

These experienced street riders have put in long hours to get to this level of competency. If you want to achieve the same level, get to a racetrack to accelerate the learning curve. The constant repetition of corner after corner all day long will drill the reflexes into your mind and body, making you ready to react with instant control when needed on the street. It's my

You can bet this isn't the first time these riders have attacked this corner. The confidence for this lean angle comes from multiple runs through the same debris-free corner. Jack Beaudry

Racing is a lot less polite than track days. If racing is your ultimate goal, a few track days would be a perfect way to ease into the sport. Mark Miller

track time that allowed me to handle the above incidents without thinking; just doing. That saved me during incident one and kept me from losing my head in incident two.

Even experienced street riders who have instinctive control need to get to a track to learn their limits. I'm talking about both their personal and their machine's limits. On the street, you always ride with some margin in reserve for the unexpected. On the track, you can reduce that to a razor-thin margin and see what you are really capable of doing.

I work with hundreds of track virgins every year, and even old veterans of the road express awe over how much they have been missing. These riders frequently comment about how they thought they were riding at the limit before

getting on a track only to find that they were not even close. After a few track days, you will gain an accurate feel for the true limits and have that additional knowledge ready to draw on in an emergency.

I have a lot more arguments about why you should get to a track day but I'll save them for the first chapter. Here, I just want to present the arguments for why you need this book. This book provides you with details on how to find track days, how to prepare for them, and things to try at a track day. And since for some riders there is a natural progression from track days to race days, Chapter 6 helps you get race ready. Finally, you'll get a list of organizations that provide track time with notes about their philosophy so you know what to expect if you ride with them.

You can find riding schools or track clubs and participate in track days without this book, but if you have any questions about what you need to be ready or what to expect when you get there, this book helps answer them. Anyone wanting to attend track days or perhaps even start a racing career can use this book as their guide through the process.

The sport of high-performance motorcycle riding is a risky undertaking. Our sport is also under increasing danger of being curtailed by those who want to intervene to save us from ourselves. I have no problem with high-performance street riding; I just want everyone who is doing it to really know what they are doing. The racetrack is the best place to gain that knowledge.

I don't want the increasing number of single-vehicle crashes by motorcyclists to attract the attention of the safety Nazis, resulting in us ending up with gelded motorcycles, bikes limited in speed or power or eliminated all together by laws trying to protect us from our "insane" risk-taking behavior. I don't need people afraid to live their lives trying to save mine by taking away my toys. We need to ensure a skill base for all our motorcycling buddies so crashes are reduced, eliminated, or at least confined to a closed course and out of the public's eye. Come join me at the track and get the skills.

Crashing is a harsh but powerful learning experience. In my 20 years of street riding and 10 years of racing, I've crashed a number of times and I've learned a lot. Throughout this book, I insert short crash stories with the hope that you can learn from my experience and not have to crash yourself to gain that same knowledge. Even if you don't learn from them, they should at least be interesting and entertaining. Let's all never crash again.

Another intense learning experience is gained from becoming a licensed racer and competing against other riders instead of just riding around the track. I've also scattered a number of short racing stories throughout for those interested.

Hope to see you all out there at the track this summer.

— Kent Larson
kent@larsonroadracing.com

CHAPTER ONE

WHY RIDE ON A TRACK?

This first chapter is a philosophical look at the sport of high-performance motorcycle riding and racing. If you are not in the mood for philosophy right now, skip to Chapter 2 and start soaking up practical information and helpful instructions for getting into track riding. Come back here when you've got time to relax and reflect.

She may look all sweet and innocent just sitting there, but don't let that fool you. Start her up and she can be more trouble than Melanie Griffith in Something Wild. *Jack Beaudry*

Bad Influences From Italy

Every time I started my 1995 Ducati 916, I knew I was in trouble. It would thunder to life and growl with deep-throated intensity. Trembling and quivering with excitement, the bike would wait for me like a coiled jaguar ready to pounce.

The excitement was infectious. When it was running, I couldn't get near the 916 without my pulse starting to race. I'd feel a click somewhere deep in my brain as my inhibitions fell away. I couldn't leave the driveway without committing petty misdemeanors. I couldn't ride that bike for 15 minutes without my behavior escalating up to felonious.

Job Interviewer: "Have you ever been convicted of a felony?"

Answer: "Convicted? Why, no. I've never been *convicted* of a felony."

Every commute to work on that bike was an exercise in restraint, one I usually failed to complete. She (my 916 was a girl for some reason) had a telepathic link to my hind brain through which she would transmit a nonstop litany of naughty suggestions. "Why so slow, Kent? We can go faster. I *want* to go faster. Come on, let's go. Let's go, go, *go!*"

She was always ready. Just a twitch of my throttle hand would unleash gobs of torque. "Now? Yes! Now! We're off! Yeah!" She would purr, growl and scream with pleasure only to be shut down as I completed a pass and returned to the flow of traffic. "No? Not now? Well, okay. But I'm ready, Kent. I'm ready right now. Should we go now? Come on, let's go. Let's go, go, *go!*"

I'd have arm pump by the time I got to work—not from trying to hold onto the bike but from having to check my desire to roll open the throttle. My right arm would constantly flex the entire trip as the desire-for-pleasure half of me tried to open the throttle and the want-to-stay-out-of-jail half fought to keep it closed.

The 916 could only put up with this abuse for a few months. She was unsatisfied nearly every ride. She soon

The 916 being treated right and allowed to run free at Blackhawk Farms Raceway. Jack Beaudry

took to starting reluctantly or not at all. Multiple trips to the shop for therapy would get her going again for a bit but she would always return to the same state of uncooperative depression.

Finally, I resolved to leave her parked unless I could treat her right. That meant getting to the racetrack where she could stretch her legs. We headed up to Brainerd, Minnesota, to get our race license with the Central Roadracing Association (CRA). I wasn't about to race my $16,000 motorcycle even though the CRA rules allowed first-time novice racers to run up to 750-cc inline fours and 1000-cc twins. Sure, my 916-cc twin-cylinder Ducati qualified, but putting that bike on the track for my first race would have been just plain stupid. I'm not a complete idiot.

No, I wasn't going to race the 916. I was just going to use it for the race school. Once I finished practice laps and a new-rider mock race with the 916, I would have my novice license. After that, I was going to just use the 916 during practice sessions for cheap track time (at that time, in 1995, CRA licensed racers could get all-day Friday practice for $40). Any racing would be done with my buddy's Suzuki GS500 race bike. He was going through the licensing class with me, and we planned on sharing the GS that summer.

I'M SURE, DESPITE ALL EVIDENCE, that my Idiot Percentage (IP) falls somewhere under 50. At least half the time I'm awake, I'm not being an idiot. I'm not being an idiot while just sitting quietly watching other people race, right? That builds up a lot of non-idiot time right there. If I were a complete idiot, I'd have an IP of 100. My non-idiot time adds up when I'm not actively doing something or talking to someone. For example, watching TV, reading a book, or riding in the passenger's seat listening to the radio all allow non-idiot moments to accumulate. Like most of us, these passive moments are sure to bring my IP down below 50. But then, we are usually too biased to accurately rate our own IP so I'll have to wait on the IP Assignment Board's ruling to be sure.

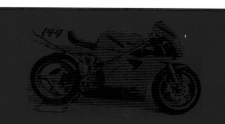

You may be wondering why "expert" is in quotes. Be aware that it's really not that hard to qualify for an "expert" license with most racing clubs. Don't expect someone to be a perfect rider just because there is a white "expert" plate on their bike instead of a yellow "novice" plate. Experts typically have fewer Idiot Moments Per Lap (IMPL) than amateurs, but they still have them. Some riders with "expert" plates simply qualified for the status by meeting some club's criteria but still don't have what I would consider expert control of their bike. Stay sharp. Don't get caught up in another rider's Idiot Moment just because you saw the white number plates and relaxed.

During the on-track class time, a white-plated "expert" racer led us around (see sidebar above). He started slowly, showing us the good line through each corner, then ratcheted up the pace a bit each lap. Soon it was just his Suzuki GSXR750 and my 916 ripping around the track like we were tied together with a 3-foot rope. Each time we started down the front straight, he'd look back and I'd give him a wave or a thumbs-up to let him know I was just fine and ready to step it up.

Halfway through the second practice session, I had my first on-track Idiot Moment. I'd been following the instructor around thinking how his bike was probably about the same weight and power as my bike. Anything he did with his bike, I should be able to do with my bike, right? See any flaw in that thinking?

We ran through turn 1 wide open at about 170 mph. We downshifted and took turn 2 at about 140, then hit the brakes and dropped two more gears on the way into turn 3. Once settled in at full lean, he looked back over his shoulder and saw me still playing his shadow. He gave a little shrug, turned back around, and was gone! "Holy crap!" I thought as I twisted my own grip trying to stay with him. Then, "Aw, crap!" as the rear wheel spun out from under me and I landed on my back.

It took me a few seconds to decide that I should let go of the throttle grip and try to get a bit of separation from the bike. I jumped the curb and skittered through the grass while watching my bike dig a handlebar and launch straight up into the air. It came back down on the gas tank and left grip. The tank was the first piece to eject as the bike rolled again and again, spreading out parts like a $16,000 yard sale.

On-Track Crash One, Lessons Learned:

1. Don't assume anything they can do, you can do. The other rider may be on a lighter bike with better suspension setup and better tires. That other rider may just simply be a better rider. There are too many variables making up each bike-and-rider package. The only thing you can learn from someone else's lap time is the fact that it is possible to go that fast. It doesn't mean *you* will ever go that fast. You may never find the perfect setup discovered by that other rider.

2. Never come to the track with a bike you can't leave in a smoldering heap outside turn three. If it's a bike you can't bear to lose, leave it at home.

Shirts over leathers can mean many things. The orange T-shirts here identify North East SportBike Association's "Control Riders" while the Central Roadracing Association uses orange shirts to designate "Pumpkins"—as the first time racers are affectionately known. Jack Beaudry

One of my former race bikes ridden by John Gateley at Brainerd International Raceway, Minnesota. A Suzuki GS500 race bike is a perfect first bike to bring to the track. Tony Marx

My 2000 Honda RC51. The bodywork is one of a kind and could not easily be replaced if damaged. I really should stay off the track and street with this bike. But what fun would that be? Kent Larson

a new tank, clip-on, and race bodywork, she was again ready to run around the track growling and purring with pleasure.

After a few years of track day duty, I sold the 916 to a friend only to buy her back after he moved on to a Ducati 996 and started neglecting my old companion. My 916 came back home with new wiring and an upgraded voltage regulator thanks to the thorough troubleshooting work of her temporary owner. Even with this theoretical new reliability, I still never returned her to the cruelty of daily commute duty. She remained my dedicated track bike up until it started sounding like a gremlin was pounding on the inside of the cases with a ball-peen hammer whenever I lugged the engine. I'm told that's the sound of a bottom end bearing going oval.

Why the Track?

Contrast a Sunday morning street ride with a typical motorcycle track day. Most likely you are already pretty certain you want to get to the racetrack or you wouldn't have picked up this book. You are a street rider with a competent, modern sportbike. You ride about as fast as or faster than anyone else on the street, but you know you still never get close to your bike's limits. As you sit having breakfast with your buddies, you think about the guy across the table who is visibly wired. He looks like you could stand him up straight and he'd start vibrating around randomly like one of those little plastic football players from that electronic game where the playing field vibrates to make the players move.

He won't stop talking! "How fast are we going to go? Do you need to worry about cops out there? I think I should put some air in my tires. They must have gotten too warm on the ride over because I could feel them start to slide. . ." and on, and on, and on.

I hope the wired guy isn't you. If that's you, then you're my pick for the "who's-gonna-crash-first" pool. I'd have a talk with you about riding your own pace and knowing your limits and not feeling pressure, but I know it's not going to work. You're still going to crash today.

It seems like any time you assemble a random collection of 10 or more sportbikers for a back roads street romp, you get at least one copy of the wired dude. Don't be that dude and don't

Nothing brings quite so much joy as seeing this sign when on a motorcycle. Kent Larson

It actually didn't take much to rebuild the Ducati. Having the tank crush and clip-on snap off was a blessing. These components took the hit for the rest of the bike, which survived the tumble without too much structural damage. With

be near him when he's going down. Getting taken out by someone else is worse than crashing on your own. If someone takes you out, there's all that messy, emotional relationship stuff to work out after. If you crash alone, you only have yourself to beat up.

The ride starts and a great time is had by all—up until vibe-boy goes down. Then the fun is done. There's a bike to pull out of the ditch, a companion to patch up or an ambulance to call, repairs to make or trailer and tow vehicle to summon. The fun ride just turned into trauma for some and an annoying drama for the rest. And that's the best-case crash scenario. A street crash could easily carry much more tragedy than just needing to repair a bike.

So what do you do?

You could avoid the general public rides and cultivate a trusted group of riding companions who keep enough skill in reserve to rarely crash. That will increase your fun trips and minimize the crash stops, but even then you'll still have the occasional incident to clean up.

You could go on solo rides, but you had better widen your safety margin. If you crash alone, you have greatly increased the

Riding hard on the street can be a lot of fun, but once some dork decides to launch his bike into a swamp, it quickly turns into work for everyone. At track days there are people trained and paid to handle these problems. Kent Larson

possibility of that being your last crash. Without help, you may not be around to crash again.

You could just give up spirited back road rides all together and limit your riding to the daily commute. But, come on! Are you kidding!? You got that bike to be Mick Doohan (or Valentino Rossi to modernize the reference), not . . . um . . . well . . . uh . . . somebody famous who just rides to work (Jay Leno? The suicidal "mod" from Quadrophenia?).

A 1,000-cc Aprilia and a 75-cc Aprilia. Both bikes finished the first 100 miles of this ride at the same time. The 75-cc rider used much higher corner speeds to "win" the street ride by a few minutes. Kent Larson

With about $750 in go-fast bits from www.af1racing.com you can turn a fun but impractical 55-mph top speed, 75-mpg Aprilia RS50 into an almost-too-fun-to-be-legal 80-mph, 60-mpg Aprilia RS75. Replace your 12-mpg SUV for a few summers of commuting and it will pay for itself. Vern Nichols

Even a 600-cc motorcycle is way too much bike to fully unleash on the street. I could sometimes talk my wife into letting me show her Yamaha R6 a good time on the track. Nick Devinck

Mrs. Larson and I give the Honda CBR929RR some fun without committing a felony at Blackhawk Farms Raceway.
Jack Beaudry

The best solution is to take your aggressive self to the racetrack.

At the racetrack you can have the same group of buddies to ride with—if you convert them, too. You can have the same break-time conversations and playful on-the-bike interactions. Only now when someone crashes there's a staff of people who were paid or who volunteered to take care of the bike and rider. It's not your problem.

You'll still get copies of vibe-boy showing up on track days just as frequently as they do on general, open-to-the-public rides. Make sure to give them the same healthy margin at the track that you would on the street. But as long as you stay away from them on the track, they are someone else's problem.

You are also able to amp it up a notch and explore the limits of your riding abilities under the relative safety of the closed course and expert supervision. On the street, you had better be riding at only eight-tenths or less to account for the unknown around any bend. On the track you can step up to ten-tenths because the unknowns are minimized.

The racetrack allows you to dial in yourself and your bike much more quickly than riding on the street. On the track, you get to see the same corner every minute or two. Not the occasional similar corner but the exact, same corner. Each time through you can try a slightly different line, brake a little later, come on the gas a little earlier or make some other small change and evaluate the outcome. Because it's the exact same corner, you can slowly focus in on a perfect plan for that corner and then start seeing how consistently you can execute that plan. When you can hit it exactly the same every lap, you know your quest for total control of your bike is complete.

Little Versus Big

Now for some Great Advice That Nobody Is Going To Use: *Get a little bike for your first track outing.*

I know that earlier I described how I picked a big sportbike to become my first dedicated motorcycle for the racetrack. You may think, "I need my 1000-cc acceleration and triple-digit

Riders wait to prove their skills at Mid-America Motorplex.
Jarel Jensen

top speeds! That's why I bought that bike. Am I supposed to just sell it?"

No, no, hang on. I'm just advising you to get a small bike for your first track bike. Once you learn to ride, go back to the big bike. As a fast street rider, you may think you know how to ride, but odds are your skills aren't as advanced as you think they are. Most street riders are shocked to find how much higher the bar is set when they hit the track for the first time. It's the rare 5 to 10 percent who come to their first track day and demonstrate competence right off.

It is rarer still to find someone with a bike making 100 horsepower or more who can actually learn to ride well using that bike on the track. In my experience, the higher the horsepower, the longer it takes to learn. Some people can overcome the handicap of high horsepower but most will stagnate into permanent screamer-parker syndrome.

Two really fast riders on very slow bikes. Any first-time track day rider would be hard pressed to hang with Drew Jager's 60-hp GS500 no matter how much horsepower they are packing, but Darrel Ion hangs with him on a Yamaha SRX600 Single. Brian J. Nelson

The bike most responsible for contracting screamer-parker syndrome. You almost can't help being a screamer-parker on a Hayabusa. You're not going to make up time in the corners with that Suzuki. Jack Beaudry

You see the screamer-parker pack every time motorcycles hit the racetrack. This group relies on their straight-line speed to compensate for lousy cornering ability. They scream down every straight just to park it in the corner. The most common complaint I get when control riding for the Northeast Sportbike Association (www.nesba.com) is about screamer-parkers. The good Suzuki SV650 or Aprilia RS250 pilot will gripe about all the screamer-parkers on 600s or bigger. The accomplished rider on a 600 will complain about the 1000-cc screamer-parkers.

The quickest cure for screamer-parker syndrome is to be on a bike that can't scream. You are forced to carry corner speed if your bike can't make up lost time in the straights. A small bike has one other huge benefit for the first-time track rider: it lowers expectations. When you hit the track on a 45-horsepower GS500 or a 65-horsepower SV650, nobody expects you to hang with the latest 600s or liter bikes.

On a little bike, you are free to concentrate on learning to ride without having to defend your manhood. It's when you have the best equipment and still get left behind that you are forced to admit the problem is you and not your bike. That's a blow some egos cannot handle.

All too often first timers at the track realize they can't run the pace of their buddies without riding well beyond their comfort level. Those really fast street riders sometimes learn that their friends really were riding at about 80 percent on the street when matching their 100 percent pace. About half the riders presented with this new awareness notch it down and start working with someone to improve their skills. The other half continue to ride over their heads and either crash or—with enough good luck—make it intact through a panic-filled afternoon.

Crash or not, the panic group isn't going to get any better unless they can admit to themselves and their friends that they need to slow down and learn some skills. Not surprisingly, it's more often female riders who can accept this blow to their "manhood" and get the help they need to improve their riding. The riders who can't accept the demotion from top dog are the ones

Female riders are a small percentage of the racing and track day participants, but you find a few at every outing. Ladies, don't be worried about coming out. You'll get plenty of support and will always find female role models with whom to ride. Laura Holland looks for the limits of traction on her Aprilia RS250. Jack Beaudry

Dawn Roberts tips into one in front of a pack of testosterone-crazed adrenalin junkies. Don't worry about them. Boys really, really like having girls around. You will find them extra polite to female participants both on and off the track. Jack Beaudry

Carol Larson shows how to rail a Suzuki SV650 around the track at Blackhawk Farms. Jack Beaudry

who start missing half their track time because they fell asleep or needed a break or missed the call or some other excuse that keeps their bike parked. That's the first and last time you see them on the racetrack.

Unless you truly are the fastest thing on two wheels, do yourself a favor and either bring a heavy heap of humility or a bike that you can blame for your "embarrassing" lap times. There is no reason to be embarrassed by slow lap times. Needing to be slower than some other rider to be comfortable isn't a problem; it's just reality. There's always going to be someone faster. The quickest way to improve is to be relaxed and comfortable. It's hard to learn or improve when stuck in a constant state of panic.

If you need a slow bike for an excuse, by all means bring one. Even if you don't need an excuse, bring a slow bike anyway. Leave your big street bike in the garage until you've mastered cornering the little bike at its limit. If you are typical, you will learn faster on a little bike. Watch any Amateur Middleweight club race

(600-cc inline fours) and you have plenty of evidence that some riders never learn to corner when they can mask their poor control with excess horsepower.

There are hundreds of fully depreciated little race bikes around. The CRA, CCS, CMRA, MRA, and WERA racing clubs all have a classifieds forum where you can find fine little well-sorted machines for next to nothing. Just Google or Yahoo "Motorcycle Roadracing," and you can find the site for most of the racing clubs around the United States. A nice GS500 or EX500 race bike can easily be had for around $1,000 or less. For $3,000 or less, you can get a three- or four-year old Suzuki SV650 race bike with some good race bits. Suzuki only pays contingency (contingency is cash or product credits paid to riders who win races using a sponsor's product) for bikes less than three years old so the fast guys need to stay current and the older race bikes' values drops significantly.

Since these bikes have already been fully depreciated before you bought them, you can ride them for a year and still

I hope one of the riders heading out onto Mid-America Motorplex will soon be you. Jarel Jensen

get near what you paid when it's time to pass them on to the next track day rookie. Leave that $8,000 to $12,000 machine in the garage. Come to the track with a cheap, disposable low-horsepower bike and learn how to ride. Once you've mastered pushing a 70-horsepower bike to its limits, you can pass it on to the next guy and start bringing your 120-plus horsepower baby to the track and show it a good time.

I believe so much in the start-on-a-small-bike philosophy that I'm trying to set up a nonprofit organization dedicated to supplying well-sorted small-horsepower bikes to new track riders. The hope is to get 20 to 30 good starter bikes donated from manufacturers, racers, track day pros, and other generous souls who will get a tax write-off instead of trying to sell their nearly worthless old machine. These will go to new track riders who want to get to the track but can't risk their street ride. To

learn more, help out, make donations, or sign up on the bike waiting list, go to www.larsonroadracing.com.

The mainstream public looks upon our sportbike hobby as stupid, pointless, risky behavior. There's a trend in America toward deciding what is and what is not acceptable behavior, then passing laws to limit the freedom of others to choose for themselves what risks they want to take.

I've never been a smoker and I don't particularly like having smokers around. However, I'm still vehemently opposed to the new laws being passed everywhere that ban smoking in all bars and restaurants and even on public beaches. What happened to the concept of the free market? If there is a demand for smoke-free bars (which there is), they will pop up on their own to fill the demand. If an owner wants to keep his bar a smoking area, he should be free to make that decision and lose all the potential nonsmoking business to a bar that decides to go smoke-free.

I used to give smokers a hard time until I noticed that I sounded just like the annoying friend/relative/stranger talking to me about sportbikes and track days. "Why do you do that? It's not good for you, you know. You could get injured or die. Is it really worth the risk you are taking?"

Hey, if the pleasures of smoking are worth the risks of cancer and early death, then by all means keep smoking. I'm not about to impose my value system on your life and would like you to extend the same courtesy to me.

We must all be ambassadors for our sport. We must try to bring those riding-over-their-heads squids with us to our next track day. Drag them to the track so they can learn to ride in a safe setting with trained emergency care specialists and ambulances ready. Let them see real riding and have them learn the limits without getting embedded in a guardrail or crushed by an oncoming SUV in the process.

I'm constantly surprised that we are still able to walk into a dealership and ride away on a machine capable of going 180 miles per hour and legally use such a machine on public roads. I don't know why this freedom still exists in our increasingly protective society, but I do know having riders attempt to use even a fraction of a modern sportbike's potential in public is ultimately going to lead to such bikes being outlawed. I still want the power to run a quarter mile in under 10 seconds and the ability to go from 60 to 100 mph in a few seconds. I still want to ride my CBR929 or RC51 on the Wisconsin back roads and public roads such as Deal's Gap, Georgia's highway 60, or the Texas hill country tarmac.

If we don't police ourselves and get the wild squids and in-your-face stunters off the streets and onto the racetracks, someone is going to take steps to save us from ourselves. It's not that big a step from protecting the public from the "evil" smoker to protecting the public from the uncontrolled "crotch rocket" pilot.

I hope you picked up this book in the fall or early winter. Not because it's going to take a long time to read; it's a pretty quick and easy read. It's just that you might need a few months time to work double shifts and get your bank account plump. If I do my job right, you are going to spend a lot of next summer at the track. The travel, tires, and track fees could run you $500 per outing. Factor in some expert instruction and a weekend could run into a few thousand dollars.

Is it worth it? Yes! You are never going to get all you can out of your bike without getting to the track. As long as you keep your ego in check, one day at the track and you'll be hooked. I hope this book prepares you to get the most out of your first day on the track and serves to pull you into a lifelong addiction.

Thanks for giving me the soapbox. Now let's go ride!

CHAPTER TWO

RELAX

Cornering, to me, is what motorcycling is all about. Any monkey can twist the throttle and hold on. The art is in the curves.

Cars crash through a corner; their chassis flex, their drivers are thrown to the side, stuff designed to support weight vertically gets strained laterally. Cornering on four wheels is a fight with physics.

Compared to cars, cornering on two wheels is pure poetry. Even a slow romp through a set of curves is ballet with a bike.
Jack Beaudry

In contrast, cornering with a motorcycle is pure poetry. Everything leans into the task and works together. The lateral and vertical forces produce a sum that stays perpendicular to the seat. With the exception of the shearing forces (primarily isolated between the tires and the road) the rider and bike continue to feel a force very similar to the force produced by gravity when everything was vertical—it is just somewhat stronger. Cornering on two wheels is a beautifully balanced dance with gravity.

That is, if everything goes right.

Riding at the racetrack helps you learn the skills needed to keep everything going right. Some of the skills you need are bike maintenance and proper suspension setup, but most of the skills are about controlling your bike. The only place to quickly master control of your bike is at the track.

It doesn't even matter what type of bike you have. From the Harley-Davidson Road King to the latest Kawasaki ZX-6RR, you should get to the track and find out what your bike will do at the limits of traction. I once watched a Road King smack down a floorboard and slide sideways across the track during a California Superbike School event at Road America. The rider got back up on the wheels just before leaving the track. After a fairly fast and bumpy ride—he was doing a good impression of a rodeo cowboy on a bull—he got it steered back to the track and continued his day.

I'm sure he reconsidered ever taking that bike to the racetrack again, but I'm glad he found that limit at the track instead of hitting it in traffic somewhere. The lumpy, grassy runoff was much kinder than oncoming traffic. If you want to find your bike's limits, be sure to get to the racetrack. The street isn't the place to slide a tire.

The limit of traction is somewhere most of us aren't ready to go. Stay away from that edge unless you are mentally prepared to be out there beyond the limits of traction. This book isn't a manual on how to ride at the limit. Plenty of other books are available to get you ready to push that far. Before you attempt to find the

Initial turn-in should be a smooth transition from braking to turning. If you watch the best riders enter a turn, the front end dives on the brakes and stays compressed all the way to full lean. Braking forces are eased off as cornering forces increase without a noticable bounce or bobble. Jack Beaudry

When appropriate, the throttle is opened. Sometimes this happens even before the apex or even before brakes are fully released. As power is rolled on, weight shifts from the front to the rear and the forks start to extend. Jack Beaudry

absolute limit of traction, get one of these how-to-ride books and study the concepts. Visualize one or both wheels breaking loose and what your proper reaction should be. Get a mental moving picture of you handling the situation. *Know* what you are going to do before it happens.

Common recommendations for how-to-ride books include *A Twist of the Wrist* and *A Twist of the Wrist II* by Keith Code, *Total Control* by Lee Parks, and *Sport Riding Techniques* by Nick Ienatsch.

My First Ride at the Limit

I had my first controlled slide at Road America in 1997 during a track day with Team Hammer Suzuki. I rode my 1996 Honda CBR900RR and quickly found out how really different this track stuff was from street riding. My first session on the track let me know the little peg feelers had to go. When I was riding street, the 2-inch bolts only rarely hit the asphalt and never touched during turn-in. At the track, I couldn't complete my flick because the feeler would slam into the

track before I got to the lean angle I wanted. I also had to park it around the carousel because I was digging the peg in so hard I was worried about levering the rear wheel off the ground.

After removing the peg feelers, I still dragged the peg in the carousel but without any pressure on it. I could ride as fast as I wanted with the peg lightly skittering across the pavement. Removing the feelers also helped with turn-in. I could now flick over to the angle I wanted without the annoying *whack!* to distract me before I was on my knee.

Note: Don't you dare use these next few paragraphs as your total at-the-limit riding instruction. Go buy the proper books and get it as presented by Code, Parks, or Ienatsch. Use the following information at your own risk. If you think I'm telling you all you need to know and you crash because you don't know enough, it's your fault, not mine.

During lunch, I had a fortunate conversation with my friend Vern. Vern and I started discussing the "survival instincts" section from one of Code's *Twist* books. We were commenting on how the

As the bike is picked up after the apex, the rear tire contact patch grows and more power can be applied without breaking traction. Jack Beaudry

Always look well through the corner. Concentrate on where you want to go, not where you currently are. Now that this corner is behind us, we can be reviewing the plan for the next turn. Jack Beaudry

Paul Larson puts a 1996 Honda CBR900RR through its paces at Blackhawk Farms Raceway. Jack Beaudry

action prompted by your survival instinct is often exactly the opposite of what you need to do on a racetrack.

Take the front-end push for example. Code says that when the front pushes due to rolling off mid-turn, it's because you're loading the tire with more weight than it can hold in the corner. When you feel the push, your instinct is to shut off the throttle, which only weights the front more and causes a low side. The proper response is to get on the gas and shift some weight off the front tire. We were joking about how the proper response for all problems seemed to be "get on the gas."

Front end pushing? Get on the gas!

Tank slapper? Get on the gas!

Rear end spinning? Get on . . . no wait . . . hold steady throttle. Don't roll on but don't shut off. At the same time, steer into the slide.

We went out on the track with me chuckling to myself, "Yep, get on the gas. That fixes everything!"

About halfway through the session, I caught up to a lapper in the middle of the carousel and had to roll off so I wouldn't run up his tailpipe. I notched off the throttle a little and . . . the front end pushed! I slid out wide and headed for the pea gravel.

My mind gave my throttle hand a panicky "Get on the gas!" command, but my arm, cool as anything, dampened it down to a calm, slow roll-on back to where I was before I rolled off to avoid the lapper. Just as Code predicted, the front end hooked up again and I was back turning like I expected.

The brain turned off its panic alarm and I notched the throttle back off a bit. The front started to slide out and my turning radius widened. I rolled back on a bit and the front hooked up and I was turning like normal.

I was very thankful we had that particular lunchtime discussion. If "get on the gas" wasn't so fresh in my mind, I'd have been looking for new bodywork for sure.

The two-seconds-between-bikes courtesy from the street doesn't exist on the track. Be prepared to notch it up to handle the close quarters. You'll need your sharpest attention and quickest reactions. Jack Beaudry

ONE OF THE REASONS WHY I will never completely give up the back road sportbike boogie: I love the high-speed, problem-solving aspect of street riding. That's something you just don't get on the track.

On the track, you see the same corner over and over and over. After awhile, you are no longer developing your plan; you are simply trying to perfectly repeat its execution.

On the street, every corner is a new problem. You have very little time to develop the plan and take action. You need to consider quickly all the factors (road condition, tire temperature, surface moisture, type of camber, radius of curve, other traffic), so seconds later you can pull the trigger and flick over onto your planned arc. You get immediate feedback on the success or failure of your solution. Every time you exactly hit the apex you planned and squirt off to the next problem, little bubbles of satisfaction, pride, and joy burst inside your chest and spread a warm tingle through your body. Anytime you miss the mark and have to suppress a panic reaction, a sick twinge of failure hits your gut. Thankfully, the bad feeling only lasts as long as it takes to hit that next corner with perfection. Without that treat of failure, your pride and joy could not be as intense.

The fact that we are courting the ultimate failure—death—is part of what gives us so much pleasure when pursuing this sport. Let's face it, folks, operating a high-horsepower performance machine isn't as safe as sitting on the couch reading a book. We've all calculated our personal risk/reward equation and wouldn't be out there if it didn't add up to favor the reward side.

The key is to be smart about what risks you take. Make sure you really know what you can do with your bike before you start pushing the limits. One of Keith Code's books had a phrase that inspired me to print up a T-shirt to spoof the formerly popular "No Fear" (Yeah, man! I ain't afraid of nothing!) shirts. On the front of my shirt is "Know Fear," on the back is "No amount of BRAVERY can substitute for SKILL and KNOWLEDGE" with the motto "bravery, skill, knowledge" standing out in a different color.

What I'm saying is, don't just go out and take foolhardy risks for the sake of risk so you can prove your bravery to yourself and others. Instead, understand the risk you are taking and only take on the amount of risk you deem acceptable for the amount of reward you will receive when you've conquered the puzzle. This is the same approach taken by anyone participating in any "extreme" sport. The skydiver, rock climber, or scuba diver doesn't survive for long if he or she doesn't understand the risk being taken.

To understand the risks, you *must* know your limits. You don't need to find the absolute limit of traction or control, you just need to push the line out a bit so you have room enough to work and still have a safety reference.

Imagine that you are on a mountain with a flat top surrounded by fog. You know there's a sharp edge out there somewhere but it can't be seen in the fog. If you cross that edge you'll fall to your doom. You want to be able to run around and play but you can't without knowing the safe limits of your play area.

So, you use a pile of bricks to outline a box with you inside. (*Yes!* There's a pile of bricks up on the foggy mountaintop.) Now you can run around inside your box without risk of falling off the cliff; you can stop when you see the bricks defining the edge of your box, and you know the bricks will come up before you get to the edge of the cliff.

Each time you run up to the brick line and slide to a stop, you push the bricks out just a little farther. The more you run and play near the outer edge of your box, the bigger the box becomes and the more area you have within which to play.

Take the time to develop your talent, and who knows, someday you too may ride for Michael Jordan. Jack Beaudry

Think of the cliff's edge as the absolute limit of traction or control. Think of the brick line as how far you've pushed your riding up to now. You know there's probably some more room to gain—that is, you are pretty sure you can push the bricks out farther before you get to the absolute edge—but you're not really sure how much farther out you can push before you lose a brick over the edge. Lose too many bricks over the edge and you lose your safety reference and the game is too dangerous to play.

You want to move your bricks out slowly. Inch them out until you can see them start to wobble. Then you know the cliff's edge. If you push the bricks out too rapidly, you can lose them over the edge and you still don't know that hard limit.

All new track riders start with a pretty small box. They don't have much room to play in until they have taken the time to push the bricks out a bit. Each time you increase your corner speed a little, you've moved out your bricks. You still don't know where

Same corner with two slightly different lines. I refine my plan for turn 4 at Blackhawk Farms Raceway and widen my arc a few feet on the second pass. OK, who am I trying to fool? I'm sure I was attempting to hit the same line both times and just missed it by a bit. Jack Beaudry

the absolute limit is, but you've been out to the new brick-lined limit so you know you can use at least that much room.

The pro riders have managed to move all their bricks out so they teeter right at the very edge of the cliff. They can run and romp across the entire mountaintop using all the available area and usually stay just inside the bricks. They are so familiar with the limits that even losing their bricks altogether isn't a problem. They can feel when they reach the edge without needing the safety reference the rest of us need. They can ride to the absolute limit without falling off.

Most of us have our bricks moved out pretty far but still have them solidly away from the cliff's edge. When we run up to the line and push on a brick, it will usually move out a bit but not fall over. If we are a bit too aggressive at our limit, we knock a brick over the edge and can be in danger of falling ourselves.

On the street, we shouldn't even try to push on the bricks. The street is not an isolated mountaintop with well-defined edges. We don't want to mess with the edge when some unknown factor can make us trip. On the track, there are fewer unknown factors to mess with us. We can run around right at the edge of our brick box comfort zone without worrying about a stumble.

You don't need to know where the cliff's edge is located, but you always need to know where your safety reference is located. As long as you stay within your reference, you won't fall off the cliff.

When I presented this metaphor to my good buddy Vern, he pointed out that there are two lines he keeps in mind. He's got his line of bricks out where he knows he can ride without crashing. He's not sure how much farther out he could venture before he's at the cliff's edge but he can tell when he's inside his safe box and when he's messing with moving his bricks.

The other line is well within his "safe" box and is just a groove drawn in the sand. It's not as clearly defined or as easy to notice as the brick safety margin. This line in the sand defines the limit where the person controlling the bike has an important role in preventing a crash.

Some riders are done with reference bricks. They have developed an instinctive feel for the absolute edge. Jack Beaudry

Vern Nichols nudges the bricks at Blackhawk Farms Raceway. Jack Beaudry

Vern thinks that inside the sand line he can be as ham-fisted as he wants. He doesn't worry so much about being smooth, precise steering, getting on the gas to un-weight the front tire, adjusting body position, or monitoring the hundreds of other items you need to when going hard. He figures he's going so slow that the bike can take care of his bad inputs and still stay on the track.

Once he crosses the sand line, he has to pay more attention because a mistake on his part will cause a crash. He's still within his brick-lined safety margin. That is, he's not pushing outside of where he's already been. He is, however, out where bad rider inputs will put him off the cliff.

When starting with a new bike or riding on a new track, Vern spends time inside the sand-line box for a session or two and only starts exploring the area between the sand line and the brick line once he is comfortable; a smart approach we should all emulate. Every time we hit the track, a little time inside the sand line is appropriate. Make sure everything feels like it should before venturing out to work on moving bricks.

So, what are some common concerns for the new track rider?

Fear of the Unknown

The greatest source of anxiety seems to be the fear of the unknown. Riders new to the racetrack start to worry about everything because it's all new. Do I have the right bike? Do I have the right tires? Will I be in everyone's way? Will everyone be in my way? Do I have the skills to safely pass slower riders? Am I going to suck? Will the other riders think I suck? Will I remember the passing rules? What do I do on a red flag? What if I crash? What if I do something stupid and cause someone else to crash? What if I fail tech? What should I bring?

For many riders this anxiety builds the night before and makes it hard to sleep. Being well rested for your track time is important enough to justify taking a sleep aid if needed. Even some experienced track day riders tell me they need to take something such as Tylenol PM or Sominex to help them sleep the night before. Be sure you know your reaction to these drugs before you rely on them for help. Don't take anything—not even over-the-counter medicines—the day before your track time unless you know your reaction from previous experience.

Drug yourself if you must—a good night's sleep is important—but a better cure for the night-before nerves is to eliminate the unknowns and ease your anxiety. Take the time to learn about the organization you are joining. Know what to expect. Almost all schools and track time providers have a solid presence on the Internet. Use the appendix to help pick a provider. Go to their website and learn their rules and expectations. You'll most likely be given an email contact for any additional questions or concerns you need answered. Better yet, many groups include a chat room or news forum where you can talk with other members and get the buyer's view instead of the seller's.

The Rider's Manual

Most organizations provide a rider's manual to spell out all expectations of the riders using their service. Be sure to find and read this manual.

Pay attention to what gear is required for the rider. Make sure you come with at least the minimal gear needed to hit the track but remember more is always better. For example, many clubs do not require a back protector but it might help you walk away from a spill so why not wear one anyway.

Check out the bike requirements. Don't come to the track without knowing that you are going to pass tech inspection. Do your own inspection in your garage or, better yet, the garage of your buddy with all the tools and bike wrenching experience. Use the manual to tell you what the track day provider is going to inspect but don't be afraid to go above and beyond with your own inspection.

Read the passing rules, which are different for each organization. They may even differ for each riding level within a single organization. Passing rules will range from no passing anywhere

When bikes collide, bad things happen. Make it your priority to prevent collisions. Faster riders need to make safe, smart passes. Slower riders must hold a predictable line through every corner. Jack Beaudry

The flag you love to see when leading a race. The flag you hate to see at a track day because it means your session is over. Jack Beaudry

to pass wherever you want. If passing is allowed, there are usually two universal rules:

1. Be polite. This isn't a race. There's no need for stuff-em-hard or push-em-wide type maneuvers. If someone is just too good to get by politely—but still holding you up—just back off or pit in for a few seconds. Then you can worry about being able to catch them again instead of worrying about how to make a pass.

2. It's the passer's responsibility to make the pass safe. If a pass goes wrong, whoever was in back should take the blame. It's never as clear cut as that previous sentence commands, but it should be. When people get hurt and bikes get destroyed, nobody wants to accept responsibility. Every incident spawns the endless Yates verses Fania (2004 Daytona Superbike) type argument; but it shouldn't. Yates was in back; he was at fault. End of discussion. The rider in front can make any stupid mistake or bone-headed maneuver he wants. It may just be that the rider in

front is so completely incompetent that controlling his bike with any predictability is beyond his capability. That still doesn't give you permission to ram him when he suddenly panics and hits the brakes mid-turn. If you are the passer, you have to account for whatever stupid things the other rider may toss at you. If that responsibility worries you, just don't attempt any passes until you are confident you have complete control of the situation. While you're not passing, try to be smooth and consistent so people trying to pass you can do so with ease. Look up the discussion on Idiot Percentage in Chapter 5, the section "watch out for the other guy" starting on page 89 for more philosophy on the fallout when two or more bikes come together.

Read about the flags and know what each color means. There are some slight differences between organizations on the meaning of some flags. Pay particular attention to what is expected when you see a black flag or a red flag. Below are the common flags and their typical meanings. If a flag has more than one common

Now there's something you hate to see. Jack Beaudry

interpretation, that will be noted. Make sure you know the interpretation expected by the organization with which you are riding.

The first four flags are usually only displayed at pit-out (where the bikes enter the track) and control the start and finish of on-track activity.

Green Flag: Track is hot. Indicates the track is open and active.

White Flag: One lap to go. The next time around, you should get the checkered flag. The white flag is always noted as a "courtesy" flag. There is no guarantee you will get the white flag a lap before the checkers.

Checkered (black and white) Flag: Session is over. Continue at normal pace for one last lap. Be ready to exit the track where desig-

nated. Get a hand or foot out as you slow at the exit. Don't slow at the flag; wait to slow for the exit. The rider trying to draft you may not have seen the checkers and slowing on the straight could cause a pileup.

Black Flag with Orange Circle: If used, the "meatball" flag is displayed along with a rider number. The rider specified is to exit the track at the end of this lap and find out why he or she was meatballed.

The following flags can be displayed at any or all corner stations as well as pit-out:

Yellow Flag: Incident ahead. No need to put out a hand or slow down but be ready for anything. The "incident" will usually be one or more bikes and riders off the track or at the edge of the track.

Objects on the racing line will prompt a red flag instead of the yellow, but you may come up on a fresh spill that hasn't yet been escalated from yellow to red. When you see a yellow flag, be ready for anything. Evasive action may be needed. It's appropriate to come off the pace just a bit to gain a little safety margin while evaluating and reacting to the incident, but be careful not to be a hazard to a rider following you who may not have seen the yellow.

Some organizations distinguish between a standing yellow and a waving yellow. The standing yellow is displayed a corner or two before the incident followed by a waving yellow shown just ahead of the incident. During a race, no passing is allowed from the waving yellow until you pass the incident. The same no-passing rule will apply for most track day organizations any time a yellow flag is displayed; waving or not. Even if the group you are with allows passing during yellow flags (doubtful), it would be safer to refrain from passing in the area of an incident.

Yellow and Black Striped Flag: This flag is known as the "debris" flag. It is shown to indicate there is something on the track ahead. One corner worker will display the flag while another makes a pushing or pulling motion to tell you which side of the track you should be on to avoid the debris. Sometimes this flag is also shown as a triangle (by holding it folded in half along the diagonal) to indicate it has started to rain and the track ahead is wet.

Black Flag: A black flag tells a specific rider there is a problem that needs to be immediately addressed. If you see a black flag waved and then the corner worker gathers it in and points it right at you, then you are the bike receiving the warning. You should immediately put out a hand or foot as a warning to

The rider's meeting starts each track day. Be there! Pay attention! You'll hear new information and special announcements needed to keep you safe on the racetrack. Jack Beaudry

Do you know the track-out procedure? Do you know where you belong in this pack? You would know if you listened at the rider's meeting. Jack Beaudry

following traffic, move off the racing line, and report to the next corner worker for instruction. Be sure to check behind you before moving over so that you don't run into someone passing you just as you start to move off the track. The problem could be anything from a problem with the bike (loose bodywork, oil leak, someone saw your brake pads fall out) to a problem with you (dangerous riding behavior, repeatedly ignoring the checkered flag). Be sure to get off track as quickly as is safely possible to avoid leaving oil, antifreeze, or other debris on the track. Never stop on the track surface. Always get off track and out of the possible impact zone when reporting to a corner worker for instruction.

Red Flag: A red flag signals the immediate stoppage of on-track activity. You should immediately put out a hand or foot as a warning to following traffic and slow down. Some organizations will have you continue around the track at a slow controlled pace and exit as normal. Other organizations will want you to report

immediately to the next corner working station. Most clubs will have you exit the track as normal and wait for information and instructions from the track marshal. If you are riding with the rare club that wants you to report to the next corner worker station, follow the procedure for the black flag; never stop on the track surface and stay out of any possible impact zone.

The Rider's Meeting

Most track days will start with a mandatory rider's meeting. Don't skip it. You should have already read over the club's manual so you know the meaning of the flags, the passing rules, your bike and rider requirements, and so on. All this same information will most likely be repeated during the rider's meeting since it's automatically assumed that nobody has read the manual. It doesn't hurt to hear it all again.

Be sure to actively listen for special announcements. There may be a track condition update you need to know or new rules for entering and leaving the track. For example, Heartland Park in Topeka, Kansas, can be run in different configurations. One Sunday morning I got to the track late and missed the rider's meeting. It had rained hard over night and the normal turn 3 area was flooded. It was lucky that I happened to follow a rider out for my first practice session since the track now had a right-hand turn at the end of the straight instead of the left-hand turn used all day Saturday. Can you imagine the disaster if I had been even later and started my first race without any practice or warm-up lap? Everyone would have run off at the green flag and edged to the left to set up for the right-hand turn as I moved right thinking I'll be able to just run around the outside of everyone going through the left hander coming up.

Don't ever miss the rider's meeting. If you missed the meeting for some reason, go up to the track marshal or whoever is running the show and ask him or her to repeat any special announcements for the day.

If you attend the rider's meeting but by the end still don't know exactly how to enter the track, exit the track, or your proper response to a black, yellow, or red flag; get your hand up and ask for clarification. Do not leave the meeting without at least this minimal set of information.

We may not yet be ready for a relaxed, worry-free, night-before slumber, but we should be closing in on that goal. By searching the track day organization's website and reading their instruction manual, many of the unknowns that cause first-timer anxiety have been eliminated. Reaching out to the organization's public contact or talking with other riders will clear up more concerns.

Let's check on how we are doing on our list of common questions presented earlier.

The Kawasaki ZRX is one of the harder bikes to ride fast at the track. It's still a fun bike to use, but the suspension requires smooth, precise inputs. Mid-corner course corrections start it oscillating like a salmon swimming up stream. Jack Beaudry

All track schools and many track day providers have instructors to help you hike up your learning curve. Jack Beaudry

Don't bring your pets to the track unless you have someone to watch them. Always keep pets on a leash. There are too many fast-moving bikes around to let them roam free. Jack Beaudry

Do I Have the Right Bike?

Yes. Any functionally sound street bike is an appropriate bike to use at the track. If you are coming with a less sporty model, be sure to verify the track day provider has an appropriate novice or beginner's group and sign up for that level. Sometimes it's the bike, not the rider, that dictates confinement to the "slow" group. Some advanced schools and track day providers are targeted only to experienced track junkies so be sure there is a "slow" group if you are bringing a slow bike.

Keep in mind that everyone wants you to have a good time. The track day provider wants you to come back and spend more money. The instructors (if any) want to see you relaxed and confidently adding to your skill set.

All the other riders started out just like you at one time and will happily give you room to grow. Talk to anyone else in the paddock and you'll find helpful, friendly advice about staying relaxed and learning at your own pace.

Monte Lutz of Sportbike Track Time (www.sportbiketracktime.com) goofs around in the pits at Putnam Park. Jack Beaudry

Well, anyone except that dude with the scuffed up 1998 GSXR600 who constantly bitches about all the idiots parking it in the corners. He thinks that "anyone who can't do a 1:20 flat at Blackhawk should just stay home and keep out of our way." But then everyone thinks he's just an asshole, so don't pay him any mind.

Ride your own pace. Relax. Improve. You need some free attention to monitor what is going on and note what can be done better if you are going to improve. Riding over your head just to keep up with someone else will stunt your development.

If you are worried about your skills, keep to the track schools or controlled track day organizations where learning riders are expected and accommodated. Wait for your skills and confidence to build before venturing out to the less supervised open track days.

If you attend an open track day and find yourself overwhelmed, don't allow a bruised ego to rob you of future track day experiences. Take your new humility to a track school and build up your skills. If you attend an open track day and find that you can smoke everyone else on the track, take your justified pride and confidence and go racing. Winning races is fun and definitely cheaper than track days even if you don't get a contract as a paid rider. Consistently finishing in the top three will have your track time paying for itself.

My good friend and fellow contributor to this book, Pat Hahn, tossed out some great advice on a public forum for the new track day attendee:

"Don't ever, *ever* 'hurry' on a motorcycle. Go fast if you want. 'Fast' is a pace. Being 'in a hurry' is a state of mind, one usually cluttered with something besides riding the bike. Never, ever, *ever* hurry. Same goes for driving cars, too. Don't hurry, be happy."

CHAPTER THREE

PREPARATION

Chapter 2, I hope, gave you enough information and insight to confidently venture out to your first track day. Use this chapter and the ones that follow to fine-tune your approach to our sport. This chapter attempts to answer many of the common questions and concerns that come up as riders get more serious about ripping fast laps at the track.

Even one of the larger easy-up-type canopies is still only half the size of a typical difficult-up. Jack Beaudry

We address questions such as "Do I have the right tires?" and "What should I bring?" I also dropped in a little guidance on the subjects of safety wiring, rider gear, physical preparation, and, unfortunately, crashing.

It would be great to include a good-stuff list here to share the products I've found over the years to be of exceptional quality. Things such as Pit Bull stands, Asphalt & Gas knee sliders, Factory Pro engine covers, and Woodcraft rear sets would make the list. Unfortunately, there isn't time or space to include that list in this book. Since the good-stuff list frequently changes and expands, having a static list in a book really isn't all that appropriate anyway. By the time you get this book, a good-stuff list should exist on www.larsonroadracing.com. Please visit and contribute your suggestions for the list.

What Should I Bring?

For the first-time track day rider, simply bring your bike (pre-inspected and ready for a full day of riding), a good set of riding gear, plenty to drink, plenty of gas, enough food for the day, and the right attitude. Once you become hooked, you'll have time to buy and bring a shade, chairs, tools, extra wheels, extra tires, an air-conditioned trailer. . . .

For now, just bring the minimum and assume you can mooch some shade and a seat between track sessions while sharing bike stories under the canopy of the crew pitted next to you. You'll never find a friendlier bunch than the crowd attending a motorcycle track day.

As you become increasingly addicted to track riding and start spending large chunks of your free time at the racetrack, you will want to flesh out your package and start hauling more comfort and conveniences along with you. You may no longer want to rely on a neighbor for tools or shelter. There are still the few experienced track junkies who take a minimalist approach and show up riding their bikes and wearing all the equipment they need. I applaud and sometimes envy this Zen approach, but most of us seem to gravitate toward dedicated track bikes, a trailer full of goodies, and a haul vehicle to get everything to the track and back.

One nice thing about having a trailer dedicated to the task is that you're always packed and ready to roll. At the end of the day,

Here is a difficult-up canopy. You get about twice the coverage area for about three-quarters the cost. True, it comes as about 40 big pieces and 100 elasctic loops to hold the tarp but once it's up, you and your 20 friends have a place to relax out of the sun or rain. Kent Larson

As long as you are going to pack tools, you may as well keep them organized. I use two toolboxes and keep sockets in one top tray with wrenches in the other. All the common socket sizes are in the top tray with extension rods attached for quick reference. All the common wrench sizes are in the smaller divided compartment for easy access. Tom Starbuck/ Starbuck Photography

do a quick oil change (most tracks have a place to leave waste oil) and a cleaning and maintenance inspection before loading the bike into the trailer. Then pack up and head home. Once home, you can just unhook the trailer and loosen up the bike tie-downs (to relieve the pressure on the forks and shock) and be done. Everything is still all loaded and ready for the next outing, and you don't

have to worry about storing your equipment. All the troublesome and time-consuming unpacking and repacking is eliminated.

Some people like to have a list so they can check off items as they are loaded. To me, that's a bit too much like work. I've been listless since the very start of my racer-boy days back in 1995. What I do is look around the garage and toss anything that looks useful into the truck and hit the road. When I unload the truck, everything gets put back in the same general area of the garage.

When I first started going to track days, if I found I was missing something, I borrowed the item from someone at the track and purchased my own copy before the next outing. This gave me a growing inventory of good-stuff-to-have that eventually stabilized over the years.

One person told me he keeps a computerized list that gets checked off when items are loaded. If he finds something was missing, it gets added to the list for next time. I guess my growing pile of stuff is the lazy person's equivalent of that electronic list. I could access my list anytime I needed by going out to the garage and looking at the pile.

Here is my list of good things to have with you for a track day or racing weekend.

1. A well-maintained, well-prepared, cleaned, and ready motorcycle. This includes making sure the chain, sprockets, tires, and brake pads are fresh enough to last the weekend.

2. Keys: One left in the bike's ignition and a backup left in the haul vehicle's glove box.

These pull straps are designed to grip tighter under load, but are known to slip, especially when wet. Always tie a knot with the excess strap and pull it tight against the gripping hardware. Any slippage will just tighten your knot and prevent significant loosening. Kent Larson

The left photo shows a chewed-up rear race Michelin. This is a strong indication of a suspension packing problem. You should no longer use this tire. The right photo shows what the same tire looks like a day later when it finally lets go and tosses you on your ass. Kent Larson

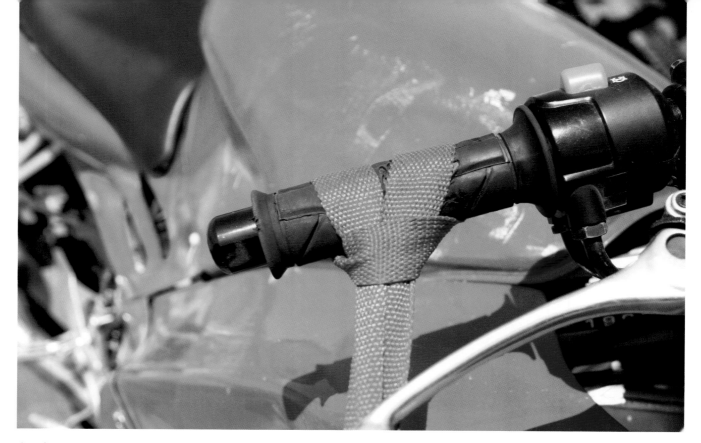

A soft-tie around your grip may seem like a convenient way to attach a strap, but don't do it. I've crushed a throttle tube with this method and have heard about bikes falling over after the grip pulls off the bar. Kent Larson

When removing your wheel, lay out all the parts in the order they came off the axle so you know how it all goes back together. Tom Starbuck/Starbuck Photography

3. Riding gear: helmet, leathers, gloves, boots, back protector, knee pucks

4. Gas

5. Shelter from the sun and rain. One easy-up-type canopy is the minimum needed to cover one or two riders. For about the same cost, a difficult-up-type canopy can be purchased to cover about three times as much area. Expect the easy-up to take about a minute for two people to set up and the difficult-up to take about 10 to 15 minutes. The extra effort pays back in a larger space for friends to gather.

6. Chairs: inexpensive folding camp chairs are scattered all over the paddock. Bring one for you and one or two for guests. Every fall these chairs sell for deep discounts. For about ten bucks each, it's worth snapping up a few extra to have around.

Don't use the axle bolt to tap out the axle; you could damage the threads, and it probably will not drive the axle out far enough to pull it out. Instead, find a deep-well socket that just fits inside the hole and use that to tap out the axle.
Tom Starbuck/Starbuck Photography

7. Tools: Start with enough tools to remove the wheels, check the tire pressure, adjust the chain, bleed the brakes, change brake pads, change sprockets, and change the oil. Make sure to bring a safety wire set (drill, drill bits, wire, and safety wire pliers). Grow the tool set over time as you find more commonly needed items.

8. Duct tape, WD40, and small zip ties. Like the saying goes: if it doesn't move and it should, use the WD40. If it moves and it shouldn't, duct it. The zip ties are always useful for quick repairs.

9. Earplugs

10. Sunscreen

11. Tire gauge and air tank

12. Stopwatch

13. Pit lackey: Bring a friend or spouse to help. This is that second person to help set up the canopy, take lap times, help get the bike on and off the stand, and share lunch with. Having a helpful, enthusiastic companion makes the day a whole lot better.

14. Lots of water and sports drinks

15. Food or cash for food

A static list in a book or someone else's checklist found on the Internet isn't going to be the magic perfect list that meets all your needs. Just use this as a starting point and grow your pile over time so that it's perfect for you.

Do I Have the Right Tires?

This is the opportunity to run some real race rubber if you want. All the top tire manufacturers offer a DOT race compound or full-on, race-only slicks to fit any high-performance bike. A properly warmed up set of race tires offers a lap time that's a few seconds better than a set of street rubber or at least gives a bigger safety margin at the same lap times. On the racetrack, you can warm up race rubber properly and actually get them to perform better than

Matt Drucker of MD Racing (www.mdracingstp.com) mounts a set of tires. Changing your tires at the track is great. For $30 or less, you can have a set mounted and balanced. If you buy a new set from a trackside vendor, they will usually give you a mount and balance for free.
Tom Starbuck/Starbuck Photography

When the tire is off, put down something clean to protect the chain from dirt and dust. If you can do a shameless Shoei plug (www.shoei-helmets.com) at the same time, it can't hurt when trying to get free helmets.
Tom Starbuck/Starbuck Photography

your street tires. Conversely, running race tires on the street usually results in tires that are never fully warmed up and provide less grip than the appropriate set of street rubber.

So, if you want to run some race DOT or slicks, now is the time. However, if you want to learn more about your street riding package, this may be a chance to test your street tires at their limit. The current crop of high-performance street tires will provide more than enough grip for a good rider to lap a lot of the other track day patrons. Just remember, your buddy with the race slicks is going to have a small advantage and don't expect to drive out of the corner at the same speed without spinning just because he is doing it right in front of you.

What Tire Pressure Should I Run?

During a street ride, you need to keep a bit more pressure to keep the tire from overheating and burning up during a long ride. A track day, with its 20- or 30-minute track sessions, allows you to lower the pressure a bit and run at optimum temperature to get optimum grip.

Here's a simple way to dial in your tire pressure: Start with between 28 and 34 psi. If the day is cooler (under 60°F), start at the low end; if it's hot (80°F or above), start at about 34 psi. Then go out, allow the tires to warm up a few laps and start pushing harder. Once you come in, take off your gloves as quick as you can and feel the tires. If they are cool or mildly warm, they didn't get up to temperature, so drop a psi. If they are really hot and look like the rubber is boiling and turning a bluish color at the edges, then they got too hot and you should add a psi or two. The ideal warmed-up temperature varies between different tire manufacturers but I've found that most brands work fairly well when my hands-on test finds the temperature just a bit uncomfortable. When I get a hand on the rubber right after I'm off the track, it's uncomfortably warm but tolerable. A tire that is too cold needs less pressure to allow the rubber to bend and stretch. A tire that is too hot needs more pressure so it does less stretching because it's the bending and stretching that generates heat in the tire.

It's very important to pay attention to your tires throughout the day. Every time you come off the track, check them for proper pressure and unusual wear. If you are lucky, a bad tire will give you some non-fatal warnings such as a gentle slip or squirm and let you know it's time to back off.

Even experienced riders (or especially experienced riders if we become complacent) can get caught out by their tires. The week when I turned this book in to the publisher, I had just returned from a weekend at Blackhawk Farms Raceway in Beloit, Wisconsin. I had a great weekend but my CBR929 wasn't too happy. He'll need a lot of work before he's ready to romp again at Putnam Park in three weeks.

The problem? Low side in turn 1. Nothing dramatic; I just sat on the track and slid to a stop. The 929 dug and broke a bar. Thankfully, the bar broke instead of launching the bike into a tumble. It needs a pipe and some new skins but it could have been worse.

What happened!? I don't crash bikes any more! I'm not racing now; I'm just tooling around doing the control rider gig for Northeast Sportbike Association (www.nesba.com). This crashing thing came as a shock to me, my bike, and my wife.

So what happened? Craig Nekola happened. Craig is a good friend and long-time race nemesis. Craig's been making me crash bikes since I met him back in 1997. In fact, now that I think about it, I'm pretty sure Craig is the reason for every motorcycle crash I've had since we've met. I'll have to work out a bill for him.

I went down to Blackhawk with one of Craig's takeoffs. He was riding a ZX9R at Blackhawk last fall and tore up the right side

Pit Bull (www.pit-bull.com) is by far the best quality bike stand on the market. You can find less expensive stands, but you won't find any of better quality. Tom Starbuck/Starbuck Photography

of the tire pretty good. The tire wasn't worn down too far—at least half the tread was still there—but big chunks and rips were pulled out all the way around the last 2 inches on the right side. I figured I could use it for a light-duty beginner's group control riding weekend. Besides, if everyone thought I ripped up the tire like that, they might think I was as cool as Craig Nekola.

Craig said the 9 was spinning and sliding pretty good around the carousel but it felt very smooth and predictable. He spent the day on that tire but decided to take it off before running at Road America. At RA the slides were not smooth or predictable. He needed to consult a suspension guru to discover the fix.

Craig was running too much rebound damping. A torn-up tire is a great indication of this problem. With too much rebound, the rear shock would pack. Packing occurs when the shock extends too slowly to recover from the last bump before the next one hits. After a few bumps, the shock is fully compressed and can no longer move. Once packed, the shock is no longer able to provide movement to accommodate bumps and the tire has to stretch and contort as the weakest link in the pile of components that are skipping along the track surface.

As long as you are waiting for tires to come back from the vendor, you may as well wire some bolts. Start with the bolt tightened to proper torque and make a mark for the hole. Plan it so a wire through the hole will pull in the direction that tightens the bolt. Tom Starbuck/Starbuck Photography

Blackhawk was fairly smooth having just been repaved. Road America was billiard-table smooth back in 1997, but lately it resembles the next-to-be-under-construction stretch of I-94 going through Chicago. That's why Craig could have fun at Blackhawk but couldn't ride Road America with the same setup. It was a problem setup in both cases but not as much of a problem at Blackhawk. Once Craig took out a few clicks of rebound damping, he was back up to speed at Road America as well.

I still figured I could save some money and use Craig's tire for the weekend. My bike didn't have a suspension problem so I could just take it easy and clean up the tire at the same time. This theory worked pretty well on Saturday. As the day wore on, the tire was looking better and better. By the end of the day, it looked almost clean. Still had half its tread and most of the ripped-up section was filed down smooth again.

At the end of the day, I took out the fast pack in the beginner group and we put down a string of 1:25s without a slide or a wobble.

Sunday started and I stepped it up a bit. The tire looked and felt fine. I started working the beginner's group and playing in intermediate. Every intermediate session, I'd go out to with one or two members looking for some help.

After lunch I went out in intermediate to work with an MV Agusta. We started dipping into the 1:27 range. I tossed it into turn 1 and looked back to make sure my shadow was still with me and that he was on the line I wanted. As I shifted my weight to turn back around, the rear tire let go. No warning squirm. No gentle slide. Just bye-bye-now, you're on the ground.

Travis (the MV Agusta pilot) said he was right behind me trying to follow my line. He had just settled into the turn thinking "Hey, this line works great" when I went down. That made him suddenly doubtful. "Maybe this isn't such a good line?"

The tire had come apart. The last 2 inches on the right side were shredded. The structural damage to the tire caused by Craig's bike didn't go away. Cleaning up the surface didn't magically mend the rips; it just made them look better. A catastrophic failure was just waiting for the right stress.

It's tempting to say the tire made me crash but it didn't. I made me crash. I'm the one who was running a questionable tire. I'm the one who didn't check their condition as the day went on. I'm the one who saved half a set of tires (about $150) at the price of half a set of bodywork, an exhaust can, and one handle bar.

Last Track Day Crash, Lessons Learned:

1. Don't trust a torn tire. Toss it.
2. Check your tires every time you come off the track.
3. Tires are cheaper than bodywork.
4. Stay away from Craig Nekola. He will make you crash.

Safety Wire

Safety wiring your bike is not often required at track days. It is always recommended but requiring it would scare off too many potential track day participants. It's not hard. It doesn't take that long. As long as you are at the track waiting for your next session, why not ask around and get someone to help you wire up the appropriate bolts?

Safety wiring is the process of drilling a small hole in the head of a bolt, running a wire through the hole and wrapping that wire around something else so the bolt isn't allowed to back out or vibrate loose. All race bikes are required to have, at a minimum, their oil drain plug, oil fill cap, and oil filter safety wired. Most racing associations also require safety wire on the brake caliper bolts, axle bolts, radiator fill cap, and many other bolts and fasteners. Even if you don't race your bike and are not required to safety wire for your track day club, it's a good idea to run some wire anyway. Safety wire serves not just to keep a bolt from backing out but it also shows at a glance that you've finished the job.

Take the task of replacing your front tire. By the time you finish, you've tightened the axle bolt, pinch bolts, and caliper bolts to the proper torque. If you safety wire these bolts, you never need to wonder "did I tighten the caliper bolts?" since a quick look confirms they are wired, which says that they are tight. The safety wire both proves the job was done and that it won't get undone by vibrations before you are ready.

If you decide you are going to wire your bike, get a rule book from a racing organization and use their list to decide what to wire. They will have a comprehensive list and if you follow their guide, you'll be ready to go racing should the desire hit you some time later.

Clamp the wires and plan on losing about 10 percent of the length when twisted. Tom Starbuck/Starbuck Photography

How to Safety Wire

You need to drill at least one hole in each bolt head. The hole needs to be placed so a wire through the hole will pull in the direction that tightens the bolt. That's pulling to the right, or clockwise. Righty-tighty, remember?

Work on one bolt at a time. Tighten the bolt to its proper specification, then make a mark on the right side so you know where to drill. Some people recommend freezing the bolt before drilling and that does help but seems more hassle than it's worth. Another recommendation I don't follow is to use a drill press. I can't get a good feel for how much pressure I'm applying with a press, so I use a hand drill. I just grab the bolt head with locking pliers and clamp the pliers to a bench. It's not pretty, but it works. You might prefer to use a press.

Use a fairly stout bit to help reduce the number of bits you snap in half. I usually use a 1/16 inch bit. Don't drill at high rpm because that will just heat up the bolt and the bit. Run the drill fairly slow but with steady pressure. You want to see the metal

steadily curling out of the hole. Slow down and ease off pressure when the bit is about to come through the other side. If it pops through too fast, you'll snap the bit as it grabs the last big chunk of metal. Ease back and let it nibble its way out of the hole. I've found it takes two or three bits to complete a bike.

Safety wire is usually required to be stainless steel and at least 0.025 inch in diameter. It's best to run from one bolt to another nearby bolt so you complete two or more bolts with one wire. If no other bolt is handy, just wrap around a convenient nearby fixed point. Run the wire through your bolt and bring both ends down to the fixed point or second bolt. Clamp on the safety wire pliers just a little past the length you want for the twisted wire. The twisted wire will be shorter than the two untwisted strands. You will lose about 10 percent of the length after twisting.

Safety wire pliers are very handy. Just clamp the wire, set the lock, and pull the knob and the pliers spin to twist the wire. Twist too fast and too tight and the wire will break. If you get in about 10 twists per inch, that's enough.

With safety wire pliers, twisting the wire is a simple pull.
Tom Starbuck/Starbuck Photography

Put the wire through the other bolt or around the fixed point and twist the ends together. Cut off the untwisted tails and you are almost done. The final touch is to bend the sharp end back on itself so that you or the tech inspector don't snag some skin on the sharp ends. Make sure the cut-wire end gets nestled up against the bolt where you can't catch it on a finger.

Crashing

Unfortunately, we need to spend a little time talking about crashing. Nobody wants to crash, but the truth is sooner or later it's going to happen to you. I know you are going to crash because you are reading this book. That means you've got more than a passing interest in doing track days with your bike. That means you have the desire to push your bike and your abilities past what most sane people would consider a safe street pace. You want to play out at the edge of the brick box we discussed in the last chapter or you wouldn't be considering going to the racetrack.

Now I firmly believe that you or I could ride a motorcycle in such a reserved and careful manner that we would never crash. We could be so slow and cautious that the back roads Harley-Davidson parade would need to pass. If we rode like that, the chance of crashing would be practically nonexistent, but what kind of fun would that be?

We have the thrill-seeking gene. You and I are not going to ride with that much reserve. We are going to push the limits and take pride in our ability to handle things on the edge. Racing and riding at the limit of traction is my form of meditation. When things are going that fast, you *must* be in the moment. There's no time to worry about money or decide if you are getting fat or dredge up any of the insecurities that may plague your idle moments. You only have time to gather data and react. Your mind is cleared of everything but the task at hand. I bet it takes the Buddhist monk years of disciplined practice to reach the same state of clarity.

Our therapy does, however, come with a cost. Because we are willing to live at the edge, we need to occasionally put up with falling off. What should you do when that happens?

First thing is to relax. Go ahead and try for a save. Get on the gas to stop a front-end push. Hold the throttle and steer into the rear-wheel spin. But once you are on the ground or in the air, it's over. Relax.

Try to lie flat and avoid rolling. If you can slide into the grass or gravel without tumbling, you will be much better off. If you are holding on to the bike, let go! The bike will slide faster than you, so you should get separation by letting go as soon as possible.

When it's over, don't jump up. If you are still on the track surface, quickly roll off out of the way of traffic. If you are out in the grass or gravel trap, do an inventory before trying to move. Try to gently contract muscles one at a time from head to foot. Search for pain that could indicate a broken bone. Don't use that bone until it's carefully examined.

This inventory will give you enough time to make sure you've come to a complete stop. I'm sure you've seen the comedy clip when someone tries to get up and run to their bike before they have stopped sliding. You don't want to make that highlight reel.

Dressing Your Bike for the Crash

Consider getting sliders for your soon-to-be-track-bound bike. Most sportbikes now have frame sliders, bar-end sliders, and swingarm sliders made specifically for each model. Having them installed could save a few hundred dollars worth of bodywork during a mishap. Think of it as dressing your bike for the crash. You've dressed yourself that way. Why not treat your bike to some protection as well?

Most footpegs sold for racing application are hard mounted. They don't fold up like the standard OEM model. Adding a set of hard-mount pegs gives your bike's frame and bodywork another barrier of protection.

Also consider a set of strengthened racing engine covers such as the ones sold by Factory Pro Tuning (www.factorypro.com). Not only do they look great, they will withstand a lot more asphalt abrasion than the OEM covers.

With frame sliders, solid mount pegs, and racing engine covers, you've greatly reduced the probable damage your bike will receive in a crash.

Jason's Advice

A friend of mine, Jason Bishop, went through the transition from street rider to track day junkie to full-on racer boy. I asked him to provide his perspective on what was needed to properly prepare for a track day. Let's wrap up this chapter by getting his views on good gear and required physical conditioning:

Locating the track for your first track day is usually the easy part. You pick the cheapest track closest to your front door and that's that. What you're going to ride is even easier; after all, exploiting the full potential of the bike in your garage is the reason you're doing this. The only question left is, "What are you going to wear?"

If you watch motorcyclists riding on any street any day of the week, you can tell that riding gear is one of the last things to cross a new motorcyclist's mind. You see the squids all over the place riding around in shorts and shades, and on the street, they might even get away with it. But that's not the case on the track, where you won't have a choice about getting geared up. Any fool can commit suicide by riding sans-protective-gear on the street—it's a form of natural selection—but you won't be allowed on the track without proper gear.

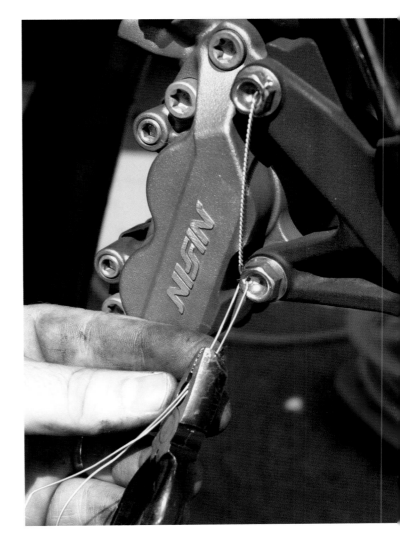

Put a wire through the second bolt and twist up the tail.
Tom Starbuck/Starbuck Photography

So where do you start? Well, the first place is the rule book for the organization with which you plan to ride. They usually have an outline of the gear you'll be required to wear while participating in one of their track days. Some also will make that gear available to you, if you're not ready to drop the cash on good gear of your own. What gear is required will likely be posted on the organization's website, or will be available as an email attachment. The flat-earthers and Luddites among you might have to resort to obtaining the information via snail mail. The wording differs from one club to another, but the list always ends up looking more or less the same.

You'll obviously need a helmet. Every club I've ridden with requires a helmet to be DOT, Snell, or Gold Stamp approved and

Once the tail is twisted and cut, bend it back in on itself to avoid leaving a sharp wire hazard for yourself or a tech inspector. Tom Starbuck/Starbuck Photography

armor, and I didn't even know what a back protector was at the time. A three-year-old helmet that I wore every day covered my head. A $40 pair of riding gloves that I bought at a local dealership protected my hands. And for foot protection I, of course, wore my trusty Marine Corps-issue combat boots. If they were good enough for the Corps, they were good enough for the track, damn it! Right?

Well, not really. Although all that gear had provided adequate protection on the street for years, it took me one session on my first track day to realize it all had to go. My leathers were heavy as hell and really limited my range of movement on the bike. I also realized how much physical work it was to go fast, and with no venting in an all-black suit, I sweat my balls off. My helmet, which was nice and comfy on the street, was now loose and sloppy on the track. My gloves kept my hands nice and warm on cool Minnesota morning rides, but the extra bulk really limited my dexterity, which can be a big deal when you're trying to go from the top of sixth gear to the middle of third and toss the bike into a turn in a matter of seconds. And the boots, well, they just sucked. The soft sole offered very little traction on the pegs and the bulky design made it hard to get under the shifter quickly.

I started doing some research and found that gear manufacturers had solved all my problems; all I had to do was cough up the cash. One of the nice things about bike gear is that, for the most part, you get what you pay for. Yes, you can find good deals on eBay or your favorite clearance sites. One of the best I've found is www.newenough.com, a great place to look for clearance items. They carry good stuff at great prices and give the best customer support I've seen. You can find some deals, but for the most part, the more money you spend, the better off you'll be. There are plenty of manufacturers with gear that meets your needs and suits your tastes, and they all make really good gear these days for good prices, so I'll just give you a few things to look for.

Leathers

For leathers, you really want a one-piece suit. Manufacturers know that for the most part these suits are going to the track, and they include features that will improve your day at the track in every way. I personally won't buy a suit unless it's fully perforated; trust me, if the temps are any higher than 60 degrees, you'll want it. You should also look for Lycra stretch panels behind the knees and the inside of the elbows to improve range of motion. You'll

a full-face design. You'll need a leather riding suit. A one-piece suit is preferable because it provides the greatest amount of protection in case of a spill, but most clubs allow a two-piece as long as it has a full-circumference zipper to join the pants to the jacket. Riding boots are next. Usually the only requirement is that the boots are constructed of leather and completely cover the ankle. And last, you'll need a pair of leather, gauntlet-style gloves that completely cover the wrist. Take it from me, a guy with one of the goofiest-looking fingers you'll ever see, you don't want to skimp on the gloves. More on that later.

So what does this all mean? Well, I can tell you what it meant to me my first track day. I had a two-piece AGV suit that I bought on clearance just because I liked the jacket: No venting, minimal body

need it. Some kind of mesh liner inside the suit will help you get it off and on when you're sweaty, and help you stay cool when you're on the track.

Armor in the suit is another important thing to look for. Some suits come with nothing but dual-density foam, which to me feels like tossing yourself off the back of a moving truck wrapped in bubble wrap. You want hard armor in the suit. If you've already bought a suit that didn't come with hard armor, then buy a complete set to replace the foam padding. Not only does hard armor better absorb the impact from a crash, but should you wear through the leather, the hard armor takes over and helps you walk away with less road rash.

Back Protection

Back protection is something that a lot of new riders overlook their first time out. Most suits come with a dual density foam pad for back protection, but is this really enough? At a recent race weekend, a friend of mine crashed and his bike came down on top of him. One of the handlebars went right through his leathers, through the speed hump, and would have made it to his spine had it not been for the armadillo-style hard back protector he was wearing. Without that he might never have walked again, but luckily he's fine and already back on his street bike. Is this kind of protection worth $60? You bet it is.

Gloves

I'll be the first to admit that I had to learn about good gloves the hard way. My first low side at the track happened during a race at Brainerd International Raceway in Minnesota. I was about halfway through an eight-lap sprint and was in the lead with about a five-second gap between me and second place and feeling pretty good about it. I came into a corner the same way I had the four laps before, but for some reason this time my front end tucked on me and I went down hard. I felt the pain immediately, but it wasn't until I stopped tumbling that I had a chance to take a look at the source of the pain. The crash happened so fast I didn't have time to let go of the bars and the left one came down hard on my hand, pinning it to the asphalt and dragging it along at about 80 mph. Although a better set of gloves wouldn't have stopped the bones from being broken, they might have prevented the worst of the damage, which caused the loss of the top digit of my left ring finger.

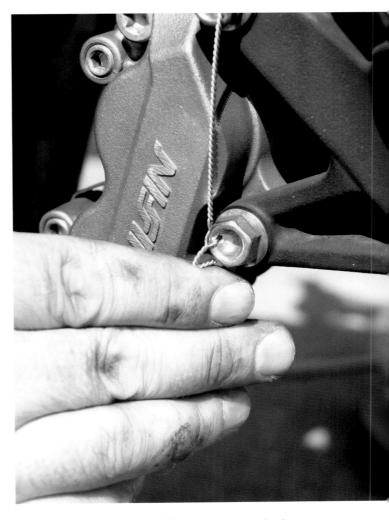

With the tail bent back and the sharp end pushed up against the bike, you can't catch and cut your skin on the burr. Tom Starbuck/Starbuck Photography

The gloves I was wearing were just leather with padding on the top sides of the fingers and a small carbon fiber plate over the big knuckles on the hand. As my hand was pinned under the bar, the pavement quickly wore through the thin padding, then through the leather, and then through my fingers. I now spend the extra money for gloves with carbon fiber or steel mesh down the entire length of the finger. Such gloves limit my movement just a little bit, but since I frequently use my hands when I'm *not* on the track, it's worth the sacrifice to, I hope, save the nine and a half fingers I have left.

A good set of gloves will have a Velcro closure for the gauntlet and another one at the wrist itself to keep the glove from coming off. The gloves with the best protection available won't do much good if the glove gets ripped off your hand. Good padding on the

This crasher refused to let go of the bike and got treated to some unneeded rag-doll action at the end of the ride. Jack Beaudry

back side of the hand to soften the initial impact is a good thing, as is, of course, something that's extremely abrasion resistant such as carbon fiber or steel mesh to keep your fingers intact as you slide down the track.

Boots

When you start shopping for boots, you might have a hard time swallowing some of the price tags you'll see. They can be expen-

sive, but again, you usually get what you pay for. The majority of crashes are low sides and the first part of your body to touch down is your inside foot. Like your hands, your ankles are fragile and a good set of racing boots offers plenty of protection, both from the impact on the pavement and the bike landing on your foot. Keep an eye out for a boot with good solid shin protection and extra abrasion resistance on the outside of the calf and ankle itself. Chances are pretty good the bike will slide on top of your foot for at least a couple of seconds and the more material you have there to keep the pavement away from your flesh the better.

Helmet

Selecting a helmet these days is pretty much a no-brainer, thanks to DOT, Snell, and Gold-Stamp certifications. When you start shelling out big bucks for helmets, you're paying more for comfort and features than additional protection. Any full-face, government-stamped helmet does a pretty good job of protecting your melon. But as you start to climb the price ladder, you'll see some trick additions that really come in handy.

Venting is definitely better in the high-end helmets, and it's really nice on hot days at the track. A locking visor is good when you're looking over your shoulder on the front straight to see if your buddy is crawling up your butt. As with all things in racing, light is right, and the top-of-the-line helmets are noticeably lighter than the cheapies.

The most important factor to consider when choosing a helmet is how well it fits. The shape of the helmet plays a much larger role in this than the cost of the helmet or its creature comforts. Don't just buy what your buddy wears; head to your local shops and try on every different brand and size of helmet you can get a hold of. An expensive helmet does you no good if it digs into your forehead the whole time you're wearing it. Different manufacturers use different shapes for their helmet shells, and you don't want to try to squeeze your potato-shaped skull into an egg-shaped helmet. If the helmet's fit is even the least bit annoying at the store, imagine what it will feel like after 100 miles of ten-tenths riding.

Other considerations

So now that you've blown a financial wad on new leathers; gloves; boots; a back protector; and a trick, racer-replica helmet, you're nice and protected and ready to rock, right? Wrong again. What's inside all that gear is even more important. I've mentioned a couple of times now how much work going fast can be. You won't really believe me until you head out there for yourself, but if you take your track time seriously, you'll want to reconsider your eating, drinking, and exercise habits in a hurry.

Whether you're talking about commuting to work, riding long distance, or tearing it up at the track, riding is about 90 percent

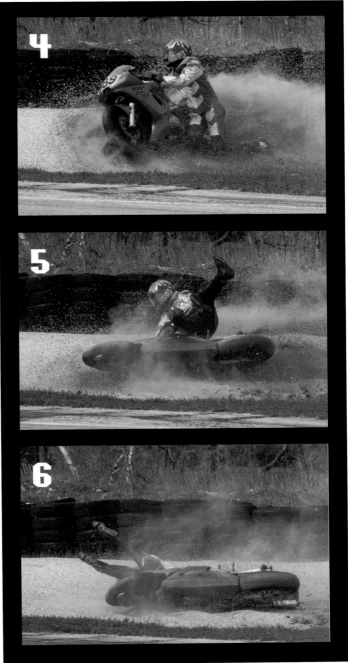

mental. I could probably preach here for days on why you should or shouldn't do this or that. But instead I'll just give you a few tips I've found useful since I started doing track days and amateur road racing.

Stay off the booze the weekend of the event. The track can be a pretty cool place to be, not just during the day while you're riding, but at night when you're kicking back with your buds and telling stories. Do you really want to be hung over the next morning when the track goes green again? You'd think this would

This crasher let go of the bike and got separation but tried to stand up before he finished sliding. Jack Beaudry

just be common sense, but you'd be amazed at how many people on the track have hangovers.

Take care of yourself while you're at the track. Eat good meals, especially breakfast, and stay hydrated. Your brain doesn't work right if its starving or thirsty and remember: Riding is 90 percent mental, so you are going to need your brain to be in good working order. Depending on how seriously you take all this track stuff, these new healthy eating habits might even work their way into your non-track life, and that ain't a bad thing either.

Physical fitness is also very important. I keep saying it, but it's a lot of work to get that bike to go fast. You're going to be jumping from one side of the bike to the other and back again. You're going to be muscling the bars to throw the bike into a turn. If you don't hurt the next day after your first track day, then you didn't try hard enough. So get into shape. Whether you go out and run, ride a bicycle, play sports, or lift weights, it'll all help you at the track. It's a lot more fun beating up your motorcycle if you don't feel like your motorcycle is beating you up the whole time as well.

I wish I could teach you everything in a few short paragraphs, but it's just not possible. What works for me might not always work for you, so a lot of this you'll have to learn on your own. If you've got questions about what gear to buy, ask around. See what gear other people are using. If you don't have a friend who's been doing track days for a while, send the club you're thinking about riding with a quick email and ask some questions. Better yet, show up to a track day and start asking questions. If there's one thing a track addict loves to do its talk about his toys. Take everything with a grain of salt and form your own opinions. Try on as much stuff as you can and shop around for deals. Your friends and family may tell you that you're nuts for wanting to do this, but riding on the track isn't insane; not preparing and protecting yourself properly is.

CHAPTER FOUR

SUSPENSION

To me, suspension tuning is one of the black arts. Sure, there is a science to it, but once a system contains more variables than I can visualize at one time, any explanation beyond "it's magic" is pretty useless. I've often wanted to learn how to diagnose and solve suspension problems, but I've never had the discipline to baseline the bike and experiment with the screws and knobs.

The 1996 Honda CBR900RR, like most sportbikes, comes from the factory with fork springs far too soft for the typical 180-plus pound rider. Jack Beaudry

That seems like a lot of work. For me it's a lot more fun to figure out how to ride around a suspension problem than it is to figure out how to fix the problem. This is, of course, the wrong approach. Think of this as me telling you what not to do.

What Not to Do

Take my latest SV650 race bike as an example. When setting up the bike, I gave it my normal suspension upgrade, which consists of simply calling Traxxion Dynamics and letting Max McAllister know what I weigh. "Hey Max, I'm 190 pounds this year. There's one set of SV forks on the way. What shock should I get?" By now Max knows not to push the top end shock with all the adjustments since I'm not going to turn any knobs anyway. Max has been treating me right since I started racing back in 1995. Anytime I took a bike from stock to race, the wheels were hung by Traxxion components.

Once I get the parts back, I bolt them on the bike and go racing. Notice that I skipped some important steps. I never set the sag or took notes on the baseline settings. I always intend to set the sag but it seems like there's always something better to do. Besides, it's only important to set the sag and get the baseline if you plan on changing the settings in an attempt to fix something. Every time I read "Before making any changes to your suspension you must use the preload to set the sag," I can just turn the page thinking, "Well, I'm not going to make any change so there's no need to do *that*." Of course, I am once again totally incorrect in my approach. Again, don't do what I do.

I had a 1996 CBR900RR street bike that tried to stand up and run wide mid-corner. The only way I could get it to stay down and finish the turn was to get on the gas HARD as soon as I leaned over. Aggressive mid-corner acceleration wasn't always possible on the street, so I frequently had to fight the bike to hold it down and keep it turning. The mid-corner standup disappeared after I

Opening the throttle while dropping in with the 2000 Honda RC51. On this particular RC51, closed throttle turn-ins made the front end push. Jack Beaudry

Sheldon Nelson hustles my former race bike (2002 Suzuki SV650) around Brainerd International Raceway. Tony Marx

did a bunch of front-end modifications. I replaced the stock triple tree with an Ontario unit that sharpened up the rake; I replaced the 16-inch front with a 17-inch rim; I sent the forks off to Max at Traxxion; and I lowered the front 15 mm on the forks during re-installation to account for the bigger wheel.

Well, the problem was solved but I don't know why or by which change. I thought about testing each change separately but that would have been a lot of work. The bike was hanging by the rafters in the garage, and getting it down for test runs and re-hung to make the next change was a disappointing prospect. For all I know, the 16- to 17-inch rim change was the key despite the 900RR list's insistence that modification would do nothing. The wise listers proclaimed there was no reason to change the rim except for the larger selection of tire compounds available for the 17-inch front.

If I was racing the 900RR or kept it as a dedicated track bike, I probably wouldn't have changed a thing. Hard mid-turn throttle is

standard behavior on the track. It was only because I needed to be more reserved on the street that I made some changes to the bike instead of just fixing the RR's ills with riding style.

My 2000 Honda RC51 had a bad push problem. Anytime I tossed it over, the front slid out. The only way to stop it was to "catch" the front end with the throttle as I fell into the turn. It felt like I turned the corner on the back wheel only, with the front skimming along just barely touching the ground, doing a lay down sideways wheelie. It felt like the "wheelie" rotation kept the front end moving through the needed arc to complete the turn instead of the pavement-to-tire forces pushing the front wheel around the corner.

I could ride the RC51 that way but I didn't like it. I prefer to ride with a lot of front-end feel. When I throw a bike over into a turn, I like to feel the squirm and grab of the front tire as it bites sideways into the pavement to provide the needed centripetal force to move

Shawn Higbee is riding on Traxxion Dynamics components and using Max McAllister's expertise to help retain his FUSA title. Jack Beaudry

the front end through its arc. My preferred style is heavy on the front end. On some advice from Jason Bishop, who pulled information from *Sport Rider* magazine, I lowered the front and raised the rear. Problem solved. I got back my desired front-end feel. How did it work? Magic!

So how about my latest race bike, the 2002 Suzuki SV650? I put it on the track and found that it too would run wide in the long sweeping corners. Unlike the RC51, I got the initial front-end bite that I like. It didn't have a stand-up and run-wide problem like the 900RR. What it was doing was failing to finish the corner.

I could do the braking, initial turn-in, and transition back to on the gas with the bike feeling balanced and beautiful. Just the way I like it. If the corner was a point-and-shoot-like turn 1 at Mid-America Motorplex (MAM), the bike felt perfect. But if the corner was a long arc like MAM's tightening-up turn 3 or the 5/6 and 7/8 sweepers, the front would start to push just after I went back on the throttle. As I accelerated harder, the front would feel increasingly vague and my line would swing yet even wider.

In April 2003, I ran the SV in three races at MAM with the Central Roadracing Association (CRA). I found that I could ride around the problem with some extra throttle.

By spinning up the rear wheel mid-turn, I could hold the line I wanted through the trouble turns. When the front end started to plow, I'd step the back end out. This kept the bike pointed in the direction I wanted because the spinning rear wheel rotated faster than the sliding front. That's a lot of fun! It makes me feel like Garry McCoy doing a two-wheel slide on his GP bike.

I managed to finish fourth in the sprint race and second in the trophy dash despite the push problem and some poor last-one-into-turn-one starts. During the trophy dash, I set the fastest lap time for my class with a 1:42.084. With my stock SV, I was turning laps faster than any other SV, built or not. Lap times didn't indicate a suspension problem but my years of experience did. I knew what a properly sorted bike felt like and that mid-turn push problem just wasn't right.

Talking to Tom Mason, the Michelin vendor (Mason Racin', thetireguy2@msn.com) about the push made me realize that I

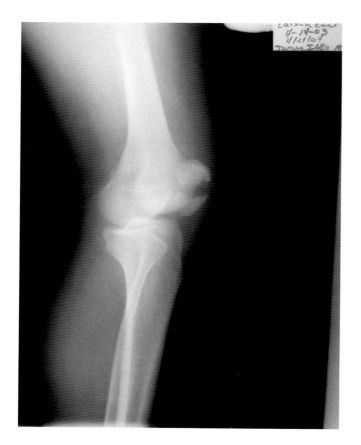 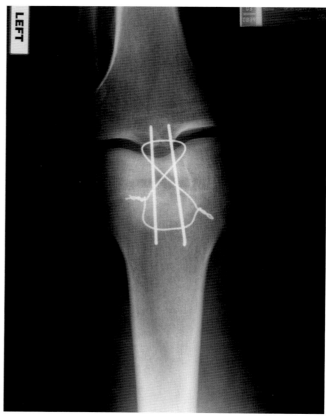

Here's what I get for pretending to be Garry McCoy. The surgery hurt a lot more than the break. You know, I think Garry's got metal in his leg right now too. Kent Larson

may be bottoming out the forks. If my weight was too much for the springs, I wouldn't have any suspension left to soak up the bumps and the front would skip. A good theory but never confirmed. I would have needed to take off the fork to remove the rock chip protectors so I could check if they were bottoming out. Besides, I was having too much fun pretending to be Garry McCoy.

My first race on Sunday ended when I plowed the front on lap 6. Another bad start had me about eighth out of the first corner but I was able to dust two more going around the outside in turn 3. I was able to keep the leaders in sight, and they had about 100 yards on me when I finished the pass for third place by out-braking two bikes going into turn 9.

My charge to the front lasted just two more corners. I rolled through 10 and tossed it into 11 but didn't get the front end squirm-and-hook I expected. Instead, the front tucked and I was sliding on my back at 80 mph. Maybe I should have tried to fix that push instead of ride around it.

I was wondering how long it was going to take to stop sliding, thinking about who had a front-end stand that would let me remove the forks, and just being cranky in general about the whole crashing thing when my shoulder hooked on something and my momentum tossed me into the air. On the second or third sky-ground-sky-ground cycle, my left knee slammed into the track and my day was done. Make that my season was done. It took two surgeries and seven months of rehab to repair the shattered kneecap.

Last Racing Crash (at least for now; there's always a chance I'll come out of retirement to crash again), Lessons Learned:

1. Don't ride around suspension problems; fix them!

2. Always take the time to check and set your sag and get baseline notes whenever changing suspension components.

3. If something hurts after a crash, don't use that something until after it's checked by a doctor. If I had immobilized my knee after the crash instead of walking around on it, I may have avoided surgery and had a two-month recovery instead of seven months downtime.

In other words, don't do what I did.

This overly long introduction to our suspension discussion illustrates how important it is to have the right vocabulary and be specific when talking to an expert suspension guru about a problem. Without being specific, all three of the bikes discussed above had the same problem: the bike would run wide. Being more specific helps the experts identify the issue.

Here is what I (the moron who's too stupid to check the sag or get a baseline setting before going racing so my thoughts will most likely be wrong) guessed was wrong with my bikes. These are, at best, good illustrations of the uninformed guesswork that goes on in the club racing pits and home mechanic garages everywhere. In a bit we will get to an expert analysis from Max in which you will learn what to do rather than what not to do.

The 900RR needed heavy throttle after turn-in to hold the bike down in the corner. My guess is a geometry problem solved by the Ontario triple.

The RC51 lost traction at the front during turn-in. Not enough front weight bias? Lowering the front and raising the rear gave me my desired turn-in feel.

The SV650 pushed mid-turn, just after coming back on the throttle. Perhaps that's a too-soft spring that lets the forks bottom?

That last guess should be pretty accurate, since I told Max to set up the bike for a 180-pound rider. That was my target weight for the start of the season. I guess I can now tell people that I broke my knee because I was 25 pounds overweight.

What to Do

Like Max says at the start of his DVD *Suspension for Mortals*, the goal here is not to make you a suspension expert. We just want to give you some knowledge and terminology so you can talk intelligently to your track-side suspension guru and have a productive discussion.

Max has been an expert motorcycle suspension tuner since before I started racing in 1995. He knows his stuff and

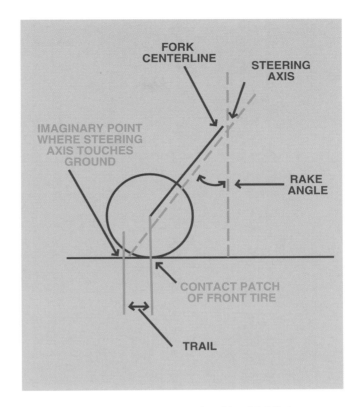

The standard rake and trail drawing. Max McAllister

Calculating rear sag starts with getting the fully extended measurement. Measure from a point on the swingarm to a point on the subframe. Don't use a point on the bodywork since the bodywork may move under the rider's weight and mess up your calcualtions. Max McAllister

Measure both the stuck down and stuck up lengths and take the average for the true sag length. Rear rider sag is the fully extended length minus the true sag with the rider aboard. To be accurate, the rider should be wearing the same gear he or she will be in when on the track. The weight of leathers, helmet, gloves, boots, and even undies need to be part of the rider sag calculation. Max McAllister

It's good to have a few friends help hold the bike when getting the sag measurements. Two helpers holding the front wheel just off the ground will give you the fully extended length. Max McAllister

isn't afraid to speak his mind or share his opinion. His bluntness will occasionally kick off an entertaining flame war on various Internet discussion forums, but I've never known him to treat anyone unfairly. I've asked him to give us the basic "what's that

knob for and why would I want to turn it?" introduction to suspension. You'll have to wait for his book for a more detailed treatment but this should get you started.

Here is what Max had to say:

This chapter is a down-to-earth guide to the fundamentals of chassis function and setup. This is a hands-on chapter that will teach you how to make your bike faster. Don't be embarrassed if you're unfamiliar with the basics. Many experienced racers aren't. This is one reason some riders struggle as novices for years and never improve. Some racers crash frequently and don't understand why. If your bike isn't set up properly, it will frighten you and you will assume that you are going as fast as you can with a small margin of safety. In the meantime, some of your buddies just continue to go faster while you stagnate. You can change this. Sometimes it's as easy as turning a couple of screws. Then you can be frightened because you really are going fast!

Let's take a reality check here to make sure that you understand what I'm talking about. Let's say your local track has Expert Racers on "D.O.T.s" (treaded race tires) doing lap times of 1:30. They are in control, but on the edge. If you are lapping at 2:10, and you are on the verge of crashing, it's because your bike's chassis is out of whack, or you are riding erratically. The first problem we can fix, and it may even help eliminate the second one!

When in Rome, do as the Romans do; when at the racetrack, do as the fast guys do, except better.

Maybe I'll be famous for that quote one day! But in reality, it's a good riding philosophy. Suspension is not an undefined science. There are known parameters that work for most motorcycles. Find the guys who are going fast and see what it is that differentiates them from you. In order to pick the brains of the fast guys, or the great tuners, you have to speak the lingo and ask intelligent questions. The following list of terms and definitions will serve as your suspension glossary.

Sag: Distance a motorcycle settles with weight on it. Two types of sag are free sag and rider sag. *Free sag* is the amount the springs compress under the weight of the bike. *Rider sag* is the amount the springs compress with the rider on board. Many variations of these terms exist, but I have chosen my own names for these terms as I feel they are most self-explanatory.

Preload: The amount a spring is compressed with no weight on it at all. Preload is measured by subtracting the installed length of a spring from its "free length" or length with no pressure on it.

Damping: The primary function of your suspension. Damping controls the movement of your springs as they encounter irregularities in the pavement. Without damping, you are riding a pogo stick. Two types of damping are compression and rebound. *Compression damping* controls the downward movement of your motorcycle (upward movement of the wheel). *Rebound damping* controls the upward movement of your motorcycle (extension of the suspension).

Rake: Angle of your steering axis, from vertical.

Trail: Distance the contact patch of the front tire trails the steering axis' imaginary point of contact with the ground. More trail makes your bike more stable. Less trail makes it steer faster. Watch the wheels of a grocery cart; they always fall in line behind the cart when you push it forward. This self-aligning effect is the result of trail.

Ride Height: Distance the motorcycle rides above the ground. This can be changed at the front or the rear (or both) to alter geometry and handling characteristics.

Valving: *Valving* suspension components is completely analogous to *jetting* with carburetors. Suspension tuners change the damping curves of a fork or shock like an engine tuner changes the damping curve of an engine. This is called *revalving*. Many times, the internal pistons are changed to alter the flow characteristics, like with the current Traxxion Dynamics Axxion Valve Kit or the Race Tech Gold Valve Kit. Having your forks or shock revalved means it will come back with a more suitable damping curve, with a more usable range of damping adjustment.

Problem Areas

A quick visual inspection of your chassis components will make sure that your chassis is adjusted to perform properly. You'll need to look closely at the following areas.

Rear Shock

Look for external physical damage to the shock itself. The main thing to look for is oil leaking around the shaft. Turn the rebound adjuster in all the way and push on the seat. We want to see very slow return action. Turn the compression adjuster in all the way, and the bike should be much harder to compress. These simple tests show that the shock is in working condition and has a range of damping force available.

Free sag is the average settling distance of the bike without a rider on board. Max McAllister

Rider sag is the average settling distance with the rider on the bike. Unlike here, the rider should be fully geared up and ready to ride. Max McAllister

Front Fork

Look for misalignment, nicks in the tubes, and damage to the sliders. Again, your primary concern is oil leaking around the seals. Turn the rebound adjuster in all the way (if your bike has

A new chain and sprocket set. The chain cannot be pulled off the sprocket. All the teeth are wide and even. Kent Larson

An old chain and sprocket set. Note how far the chain can be pulled off the rear sprocket. Note the worn teeth on the front sprocket and their wave-like shape. Kent Larson

one). Again, we are looking for very slow return action when you pull the brake and push down on the fork with a strong forceful push. Turn the compression adjuster in (if so equipped), and the fork should feel stiffer when you push on it.

Tires

Look for irregular wear patterns. Tires can tell you a lot about the function of your chassis. They should be smooth and clean with no major visible irregularities. Don't be stupid: Make sure the tires have lots of the thick black stuff they come with (when new) around the outside. This will make you go faster than just about anything else. It also keeps you from crashing.

Wheels

These should be round and straight. Two millimeters of runout is the service limit, up and down, and side to side. Inspect the bearings any time you remove the wheel. This also helps keep the skin on your butt nice and young looking.

Brakes

Check for fluid leaks by pulling hard on the lever and keeping pressure on it for a minute or so. There should be no fluid escape *at all* from around any of the fittings. Use a high boiling point racing DOT 3 or 4 fluid. Look closely at your rotors and be conscious of their wear.

Chain and Sprockets

This is simply the most commonly screwed up service item on motorcycles. Most people have their chains too tight. It should still have slop in it even when you sit on the bike. A worn chain is a recipe for disaster. Don't screw around with a worn chain. To inspect the condition of the chain, go to the farthest rearward section of the rear sprocket, grab the chain, and pull on it. If you can lift it off the sprocket far enough to see a gap between the sprocket and chain, the whole setup is worn out and should be replaced. If you pull on the chain and it fits so tightly that it doesn't lift off the sprocket, then it is like new.

Steering Head

An improperly adjusted steering head is simply dangerous. If it's too loose, the bike will wobble and chatter. If it's too tight, the bike will *track* (go where it wants on the straights) and not steer properly. Try and find an expert mechanic to assist you with this.

Setup

Next let's do some measuring and adjusting. We will use a known working baseline to set up your chassis. Then the next time you practice, you will be able to analyze how it works and fine-tune it to work even better. Note: All suspension adjustments made by pushing or bouncing on the bike should be made with the bike off the stands, on level ground, and with the transmission out of gear.

Rear Shock

The first and most basic adjustment is to set the sag on the shock. When you make these measurements, accuracy is important. Use a metric tape measure with millimeter increments (it's 2004 now, America, let's get with the Metric System!). If you have to use an S.A.E. tape, measure to the sixteenth of an inch (1 inch = 25.4 mm). You need to pick two fixed points on the rear of your bike for this: one on the rear of the swingarm (like a stand spool or the axle), and one on the subframe. I prefer the subframe over the outside of the body-work because the bodywork usually sags when the rider gets on. This will screw up your calculations. Before you can measure the sag, you must first find the fully extended measurement between your two points. Have a friend help you by pulling up on the footpegs to fully extend the rear suspension. Your bike may be fully extended already. If it is, this is not a problem. Record the distance at "full extension" on your log sheet.

In order to measure sag properly, you must take the "stiction" or drag in the system into account. This is the most common point of confusion between the

Upside down fork (on the left) and standard fork (on the right).
Max McAllister

various methods of measuring sag. If you just sit on the bike, bounce a few times, and have someone measure, you will get high numbers because the bike will tend to stop in a "stuck down" position. The method I prefer measures "stuck up" and "stuck down" and then takes the average. Get a pen and paper to take notes of your measurements, and use the following procedure.

Take the bike off its stand and balance it. Push down on your seat and very, very, very slowly release the suspension. Have another person measure and record the distance between the selected points. This is "stuck down." Now lift up the rear of the bike and let it settle down very, very, very slowly. Then measure that distance. Halfway between stuck up and stuck down is where theoretical "true sag" would be if your bike had no stiction. Subtract the average, or true sag number, from your full extension number, and you will have your free sag. There should definitely be free sag on the rear shock. Most expert race bikes have 5–10 mm free sag. Personally, I recommend 10 mm and I never change it.

Too much stiction in the rear suspension is anything greater than 5 mm; 2 mm is good, 3 mm is normal, and at 5 mm, some-thing is wrong and needs to be fixed. Take the time to inspect all the bearings and pivot points. Make sure nothing is binding.

The next measurement is rider sag. Have another friend stand at the front of your bike and balance it by the ends of the handle-bars. If you don't have an abundance of buddies standing around with nothing to do, then get on your bike (in your riding position) and balance yourself with one hand on a workbench or a pole. Have the same person who took the free sag measurements perform all pushing and measuring operations. Have that person push down on the bike and very, very, very slowly release it. Then re-measure the distance between the two points. Record this stuck-down measurement on your log sheet. Then have that person lift the bike to top out (yes, you are on the bike and have not moved during this whole procedure), and then let it settle very, very, very slowly. Find the average of this stuck-up number and the stuck-down number, and you will have the true sag with a rider on board. Next you need to subtract your true sag meas-urement from your full extension measurement. This is your rear rider sag measurement. You should have 30 mm of sag. This is your baseline setting and can be adjusted after your test ride.

You set the sag by changing the amount of preload. If you have too much rider sag (over 30 mm), you need to add preload to the spring. Compressing the spring some will make it stiffer in the top portion of the stroke so it compresses less under the rider's weight and makes the sag smaller. If you have too little rider sag (under 30 mm), soften the preload. This will soften the spring initially and allow more compression under the rider's weight so the sag is larger.

Once you have used the preload adjustment to get the desired rider sag, recheck the free sag. If your spring tops out the bike (zero free sag), you will need a stiffer spring. This may seem counter-intuitive. Why would a stiffer spring give you more free sag? The answer has to do with the applied preload. When the spring is too soft, you need to use a lot of preload to get the proper rider sag. With the spring cranked down under preload, it becomes too stiff in the top of the stroke to allow any free sag. By putting on a stiffer spring, you can use less preload to get the desired rider sag. With less preload on the spring, it can more easily compress under the bike's weight and will give you more free sag.

Too much free sag with proper rider sag requires softer springs, although you aren't likely to find this on a stock motorcycle.

Now we need to adjust the damping. The object is to get the suspension to respond as quickly as possible to irregularities in the pavement. Damping is required to control the movement of the wheel and the spring. Set your rebound damping adjuster first. It is located at the bottom of your rear shock. It is difficult to explain how it should appear, but as you push on the seat, it should return quickly, but not instantaneously. It should take about one second for it to return to the top from a hard push.

You should be able to watch the seat rise, as if controlled. If it just pops back up right away, you need to add rebound. If it drags up slowly, loosen it up.

If you have a compression adjuster on your shock, it is located on the reservoir. Set it up in the middle of its range. You can determine how to adjust it after your initial test ride.

Front Fork

Start by setting the sag on the fork the same way we did on the shock. First you need a fully extended measurement. I've found that the only way to get this measurement with any consistency is to have two guys pick up the bike by the handlebars until the front wheel actually leaves the ground slightly. Measure the exposed area of the fork slider. On a conventional fork, this will

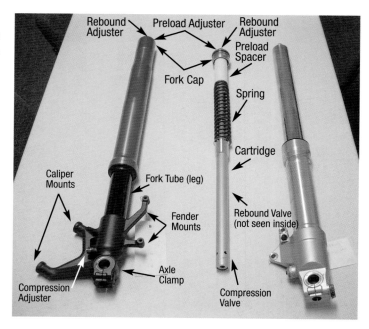

The components of a fully adjustable upside down fork.
Max McAllister

be from the bottom of the lower triple clamp to the top of the dust seal on the lower slider. For an inverted or "upside-down" fork, this will be from the dust seal down to the top edge of the aluminum axle clamp. Record this measurement on your log sheet. Follow the exact same measurement procedures with the fork that you did on the shock. The sag measurements we are looking for on the front fork are 20 mm for free sag and 35 mm for rider sag. The front fork has to have a great deal of free sag so that the front wheel may move *down* into a hole as well as up and over a bump. If your fork has too much sag, turn the preload adjuster in. If you don't have preload adjusters, then you will have to remove your fork spacers and cut longer preload spacers. Adjust in 10 mm increments. When you get close, you can go to fives. Odds are not good you will be able to attain proper sag settings with stock springs on stock street bikes.

As far as stiction in the front suspension is concerned, 4 mm is good, 7 mm is normal, and anything beyond 10 mm is very bad. There is a batch of modern bikes with Kayaba forks that can't get below that number, but also cannot be fixed and remain super-sport legal. They are the 2003–2004 GSXR1000, the 2004 R-1, and the 2004 ZX10R.

Next is the damping adjustment. The fork needs to move much faster by comparison than the shock. Again, you should be able to watch it rebound, but not as slowly as the shock. Grab the front brake and push down on the front of the bike as hard as you can. Don't release the brake and don't resist the rising action of the fork. Observe its action. You want it to rise back as quickly as possible without topping out and settling back down again. Loosen the rebound until the bike *does* want to settle back after topping out, and then dial in just enough rebound to make that settling tendency go away.

The compression adjuster should be set as softly as possible while still preventing the fork from bottoming over severe bumps or under hard braking. If you have any doubt, set it in the middle of its range.

If you do not have these adjusters available to you externally, then you must change your fork oil weight to adjust the damping. Thicker oil affects both compression and rebound damping but primarily affects rebound damping. Thicker oil increases the damping while thinner oil decreases damping.

If your forks work properly over bumps but bottom under hard braking, you can add more oil, in effect raising the oil level, to help prevent bottoming. Basically, there are two springs in your fork. One is a steel mechanical spring, which is usually linear or "straight rate." The second spring is a column of air on top of the oil. Air is a naturally progressive spring. These two springs act together to produce a slightly progressive spring rate curve. The object is to have the system be progressive only in the bottom of the stroke to resist bottoming. By adding oil, we increase the compression ratio that is inside of your forks. This helps stop the forks from bottoming.

Steering Damper

This is primarily a safety device and should be thought of as such and treated with *great respect*. Anyone racing without one might as well not wear leathers or a helmet. It's very dangerous. Don't misunderstand me, though. A steering damper *should not* be used to mask an ill-handling motorcycle. When you go out to test your suspension, have the dampener set so that it barely drags when you sweep the wheel from side to side. It should not make your bike difficult to steer in the pits. Test ride the bike and analyze what it's doing before you crank up the damper. A damper that is too stiff will make the bike track from side to side and will be difficult to steer. *It can even make the bike wobble*

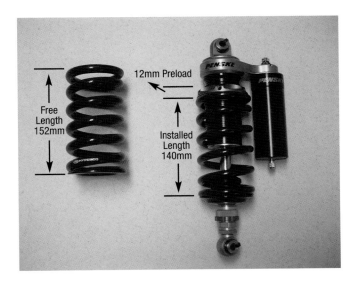

Shock spring free length verses a shock spring under pre-load. Max McAllister

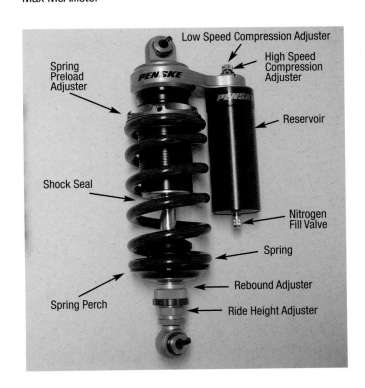

The components of a shock. Max McAllister

worse! After you make changes, always return to this base setting and then adjust as needed.

Gearing

Proper gearing can cut *seconds* off your lap time. In an ideal world, you would have a stack of sprockets that would allow you to choose

Racing Story From Kent

When I started my 1997 racing season on a 1988 Yamaha FZR400, I didn't have a steering damper and I didn't think I needed one. I felt that a good rider on a properly sorted bike should be able to handle any tank slappers or front-end twitchiness without needing a damper. A tank slapper is fixed by just staying loose on the grips and getting on the gas. I'd proven to myself many times that slappers go away after a few seconds if your bike is properly balanced. Any twitchiness you feel is just good feedback telling you what the bike is doing. Excessive twitching tells you there is something to fix. It was my belief that the only thing a damper would do is mask a problem. I'd rather feel what the bike is doing.

That opinion ended in the middle of a Lightweight Supersport race with the Central Roadracing Association at Brainerd International Raceway in Minnesota. I started at the front of the novice pack behind four rows of experts. It was a one-wave start and I got off the line well. By the time we got to turn 3, I had passed all but four of the experts. After a few more laps, I was second overall behind Sean Mowry. I could see I wasn't going to catch Sean and checking behind me down the straight showed I had a big enough gap (about a mile) to relax. I'd just won the novice race and got second overall. What should I do with the next four or five laps until the checkers?

Well, I thought, I'm still not as good going left as I am going right. I can use this time to practice my left turns and improve some. Seemed like a good idea at the time.

The next lap I tried to rail turn 4. Not bad, but I could have gone faster. Here comes turn 6, let's make this perfect. I tossed it in a bit faster than the last lap and got on the gas nice and early. I could tell I was going to go a bit wide but that's okay. Going a little wide is what the rumble strip is for.

By the time I drifted out to the rumble strip, I was almost upright again. I finished rolling on to wide open and leaned slightly left to drift back to the track proper. I could see that I was going to still be a little right of the track surface by the time I reached the end of the rumble strip, but I didn't worry about that or change my line, I would just jump the gap from rumbles to track like I occasionally do at the exit of turn 3.

This didn't quite work as expected. Turn 3 didn't have the big sinkhole at the end of the rumble strip like there was at turn

6. Wham! My front wheel dipped into the hole and caught the edge of the track at an angle. I still jumped up onto the track but I was having the worst tank slapper of my racing career.

Well no biggie, just stay loose and wick up the throttle, right? Oh, wait, I'm already at wide open throttle. Crap! Now what?

The slapper just kept getting worse as I bounced down the track toward turn 7. I had plenty of time to think but couldn't come up with anything. I figured trying to shift would just transfer the front-end wobble into the chassis as I worked the clutch or make the slapper even more violent during the momentary loss of power. As the bike started hopping the front wheel back and forth down a 2-foot-wide path, I gave a last desperate attempt to grab the bars hard mid-hop and land with the front wheel strait.

"Well that didn't work" I thought as the little FZR tossed me into the air.

Mark Foster was the lead novice at that time and he later told me, "I came around turn 6 and saw you lying on the track at the entrance to turn 7. I picked a line that didn't run over you but couldn't figure out what happened. You were gone about halfway through that race. You were out front and not racing with anyone while I was working hard to keep second place. Thanks for letting me win that one."

An old pro and great tuner suggested that I might have tried to stand on the rear brake and pull the front out of the slapper by rapidly slowing down. I don't know if that would have worked and I kinda doubt that it would. My hope is to never need to try that technique. Now I run a damper on the track.

I still don't run a damper on my street bikes. The same old argument about masking problems applies, and I'm almost never at wide open throttle on the street. Maybe I'm living dangerously, but I'd still rather feel every twitch and squirm the front end is transmitting without a damper filtering the events.

No Damper Crash, Lessons Learned:

1. Always run a damper at the track. You may find you can't accelerate out of a tank slapper because it starts when you can't give more throttle. If that happens, you will need to rely on a damper to fix the wobble.

2. Don't use race time for practice. Just race. You can practice during practice.

the correct ratio for the track and conditions present. If you don't have the right gearing, find it. It's worth more than *thousands* of dollars of horsepower. If you ride at only one or two tracks, check Internet chat lists and check at the track to find out the gearing combinations that riders of your skill level commonly use.

Jockey Check

This is my own quick test method. Start the bike and ride along at 5–10 miles per hour and assume your riding position. Lift up off the seat slightly and bounce down on the bike. It should compress and rebound in a balanced fashion from front to rear. If your bike isn't balanced, it won't work right. *Our initial adjustments are only to get to this simple test.* If the bike isn't acting balanced, *adjust it until it does regardless of the initial adjustments you made.*

Balance is the single most important facet of chassis setup. A bike that is too soft or too stiff is still easier to go fast on than one that is out of balance. If you bounce lightly, it should compress and extend uniformly. This will help you judge if the preloads are balanced. Then bounce with great force, and you will be able to see if the spring rates are balanced, and the damping is balanced. Above all else, balance is key.

The Test Ride

Now that you have a good baseline setup, it's time for a test ride. Ensure that your tires have the correct pressure in them, and head out to ride (see the discussion on tire pressures in Chapter 2). In order to make an assessment of your bike's chassis, you need to be conscious of what's going on while you are riding it. Someday when you're a racing god, you'll have data acquisition equipment to tell your chassis engineers what to adjust. But until then, you are the only suspension sensor on your motorcycle. This is actually the best way to learn. There are several things you need to analyze as you ride.

High Speed Stability

This should be self-explanatory and the easiest to analyze. Go fast in a straight line and your bike should never scare you.

Performance Under Braking

Is the bike stable? Does it squirm underneath you? Does the front wheel bounce? Does the rear wheel bounce? Does the fork bottom? How does the bike behave trail braking into the turn?

Performance in the Corner

This needs to be analyzed in three segments: Turn-in, mid-corner, and exit. Be conscious of *all* these things *within* each of these segments: overall stability, steering effort, ground clearance, front-wheel action, and rear-wheel action. That's a bunch of stuff to think about, especially when you're just trying to circulate and learn to ride. If any of these things are out of whack, they'll usually let you know, consistently, in most turns. Here's a further explanation of each of these items.

Overall Stability

The main thing to look for is wallowing and spongy action. There shouldn't be any. Wallow indicates a need for a higher spring rate. If you haven't purchased springs suited to your weight, you are likely to experience this.

Steering Effort

Does the bike track well in the corners? Do you have to fight to keep it on the racing line? Are your arms completely worn out after practice? Is the front trying to "tuck" or "fold up" on you? This is the feeling that the bike is trying to turn under on you, or have the wheel turned so far in the direction the bike is pointed that you may crash.

Ground Clearance

If you have anything dragging the ground, you have a problem that could result in injury. Some guys think they're cool because they're dragging stuff around the track. These people are a hazard to themselves and to others. If you have anything dragging, fix it! Raise your footpegs, bend in your pipe, or whatever it takes. If you lean in hard enough on a bike that's scraping the ground, you will lift a tire off the ground, and then you will immediately take its place on the pavement!

In other words, this is serious business. If you are happy with the way your chassis works, then *don't alter your ride height* to stop things from dragging. Just get the dragging stuff up and out of the way. Changing ride height alters the bike's handling characteristics. There is no way to change the bike "equally." If you change the angle of the swingarm, you have altered the way the bike will leave the turn, period.

Somebody's about to tuck the front. He's not on the brakes but doesn't look like he's on the gas either. Is he loading the front by being off throttle? Jack Beaudry

Front Wheel Action

The wheel should roll smoothly through the corner and inspire confidence. Does the wheel bounce? If it does, you need to pay close attention to the way it bounces. If the wheel is bouncing and you can't really feel it in the bars, then this is a lack of rebound damping. If the handlebars are jarring you, then you may have too much spring preload or compression damping.

Use rebound damping carefully. Too much rebound damping creates a situation where the fork is "packing down." This means your fork has collapsed and is not re-extending fast enough. This is a *very dangerous* situation. A fork that has packed down has no suspension travel left. A crash is imminent. You need to speed up your rebound damping. You may also need a higher fork oil level, or more compression damping to keep the fork from bottoming. This situation is usually set up by hard braking that compresses

the fork followed by trail braking into the turn, which never lets the fork recover. Some additional spring preload (a little!) may help this too.

Rear Wheel Action

Your rear wheel can exhibit many of the same symptoms as the front wheel. If your bike feels like a pogo stick, typically it indicates an all-around lack of damping. This condition will also cause unnecessary wheelspin on exit and tear up your tire. Wheelspin also fools riders into believing that they are going fast; that is, until some novice on a GS500E goes railing around the outside of them in a turn. Be careful about using too much rebound damping, as with the fork. Too much rebound will cause the rear wheel to "swim" under the bike side to side under hard straight-line braking. This is because the shock is packing up and the rear wheel is hanging in the air instead of returning to the ground to keep you pointed straight.

A lack of compression damping will cause the bike to pogo while under acceleration. This will be a vertical sawing motion, vertical relative to the bike even though it is still leaned over. Too much compression damping will make the bike buck or kick you in the butt over sharp bumps. This can also cause excessive wheelspin. The shock should be soft enough to let the bike squat some. This transfer of weight helps give the tire more grip.

When you notice a flaw in your suspension, note where it occurred in the turn. Was it as you rolled into the turn, was it in the middle of the corner, or was it as you accelerated out of the turn? This is critical information to help you (and a suspension tuner) decide what the correct changes should be.

Chassis Geometry

If your bike's chassis is soaking bumps properly but your bike isn't steering around the track properly, then you need to adjust the attitude or geometry of your bike. This will affect it all the way around the track.

The variables you have to work with are the fork height and the swingarm angle. Here's what each does.

Fork height will increase or decrease your trail. Moving the nose of the bike lower (forks higher in clamps) will make it steer faster, but will be less stable. Moving the nose of the bike higher (forks lower in clamps) will require more steering effort but will increase stability. Most expert riders say this increases feedback at extreme lean angles.

For most novice riders, I find the easiest way to evaluate this is to ride through a high-speed sweeper and evaluate how the bike steers into the turn and notice how much effort it takes to make it steer to the apex of the turn. In other words, how does it hold a line?

If the bike is too high in the front, it will steer in slowly and require that you pull on the bars to hold it down to get it to the apex. This condition will make it very difficult to steer the bike to the apex. It will fatigue your arms and they will feel tired after riding.

If the bike is too low in the front, it will steer in dramatically, and try and drive off the inside of the track. It will be unstable all

This sequence shows a front-end tuck. Notice how the front wheel folds in under the bike. Jack Beaudry

the way through a turn, and sometimes even on the straights.

Swingarm angle tunes the way the bike reacts to acceleration. Your motorcycle wants to squat under acceleration due to the rearward weight transfer.

If the swingarm is too flat, the bike will squat too much, and the bike will sit back and the front will extend like a chopper. This will

Still having trouble with the RC51 before the geometry change. The upper body tension is easy to see as I fight the bike through turn 6 at Putnam Park. Jack Beaudry

make the bike want to run wide or run off the edge of the track at the exit of the turn. The front end will feel light and dance about as you are leaving the turn. The result is that you have to wait to get on the throttle. This can also cause wheelspin. If you open the throttle and the bike begins to leave the turn, but after a second or two the wheel starts spinning, you may have a squat and spin situation. You should raise the rear of the bike to correct these problems.

If the swingarm angle is too steep, then the bike will not squat enough, and the result will be poor traction. This is instant wheelspin. If you open the gas, and the wheel spins up instantly, then you need to lower the back of the bike.

Here's where it gets even more complicated. Changing one end of the bike affects the other. There is a simple way to figure it out. If your problem occurs from steer-in to mid-corner, then change the front. If your problem occurs from the moment you open the throttle to the exit, then change the rear. Although there is no way to accurately mathematically describe what happens when you make a change, here is a *very* crude way to think about it.

Changing the front ride height has an effect of "5" on the front and an effect of "1" on the rear. Changing the rear has an effect of "5" on the rear, and an effect of "1" on the front.

A common example of where riders improperly change their bikes occurs when the bike steers in too slowly. Many confused riders and tuners raise the back of the bike. This makes the nose steeper, and the bike steer more sharply. But remember, in order to get an effect of "1" on the front of the bike, you have now made an effect of "5" on the rear. Your bike may now turn-in better, but you will get less traction, more wheelspin, and more tendency to high side. This is not what you want. The correct change is to lower the nose of the bike. This affects the turn-in "5" and the exit "1." Much better!

If you have no idea where to start with your geometry, look around the pits. There is no correct answer or magic formula for what you personally want your bike to do. Your personal style of riding dictates what you do with the bike. You will find that most production bikes are way off of what is generally good. Find what the range of "good" seems to be for your model of bike and start on the safe or stable side of the range.

With this information, you should have a good idea what's going on with your bike on the track. Here's the bad news: You will always be adjusting it if you want to go faster! *Do not* be afraid to make changes! You will never learn or improve if you don't. Nothing you do will make you go out and crash unless you are stupid. Make a change, and then slowly build up to your pace over a couple of laps to feel out the difference. If it doesn't feel better to you, then come back into the pits and change it back. If it does feel better, you may still want to change it back to be sure. It is easy to convince yourself you made your bike "better," because you want it to be. This is how most people get lost.

If you make a change and go out and crash, it is not because you made a change, it is because you made a mistake on the track. It's the rider's responsibility to find the limits of the bike and not exceed them. Bikes don't crash bikes; people crash bikes. It isn't because your tires were cold, you picked the wrong compound, your suspension guy gave you bad advice, or you put in the race fuel and got more power. You crashed because you crashed. Nobody ever seems to want to admit that. I have dealt with literally thousands of racers, and have met less than a dozen who just suck it up and take the blame for crashing their bike.

If you think about professional riders (they are even worse about accepting blame, by the way), they get different springs, forks, and shocks all the time, sometimes several in a day. They aren't usually just making simple little changes. If you could crash from a few simple clicks of rebound or a turn of ride height, then pro riders would never finish practice! The point is not to be scared to make changes.

Again, the goal in this chapter is simply to equip you with enough information to help you seek professional advice. It will also be helpful not to run around like a chicken with your head cut off asking every Tom, Dick, and Harry who will give you advice on what to do with your bike. Find a tuner, work with him consistently, and if you find he doesn't meet your needs, then work with someone else. But don't bounce around. Every tuner has his or her own ideas, and most think the other guys are wrong. It's no different with doctors, lawyers, mechanics, or computer geeks. Just try and limit your level of confusion.

Make notes after you get off the track while your thoughts are clear in your mind. If you are unsure about which way to go with your adjustments, your notes will be helpful to you when you seek advice. Keep a thorough log of all your changes. The next time you return to the same track, you'll be able to set up better before you get there. You'll find that a properly setup chassis will be worth more than all the horsepower money can buy.

Bike Analysis

Let's conclude our suspension discussion by taking another look at my three problem bikes. Now that we have an understanding of the basics and a specific vocabulary to use, we can make a proper analysis.

1996 Honda CBR900RR

Kent: The 900RR needed heavy throttle after turn-in to hold the bike down in the corner. My guess is a geometry problem solved by the Ontario triple.

Max: What do you mean by "hold the bike down"? Was the bike trying to stand up by itself in the middle of a turn? Did you have proper springs in the forks? Was the bike trying to tuck (aka fold up, or have the wheel turn under toward the apex)?

Kent: The bike was trying to stand up by itself in the middle of a turn. The brake and flick felt the same, but if I got on the power with a mild roll-on, the bike would try to stand up and I'd have to fight the bars to keep it turning. However, if I did an aggressive, racing-type roll-on, I could get the bike to stay down and complete the turn without having to fight the bars. It was not trying to tuck; it just wanted to stand up unless I got on the gas hard and firm. The problem occurred with stock springs and stock setup for the 1996 CBR900RR as delivered by the dealer. The problem went away after changing the triple to the Ontario unit, putting on a 17-inch front rim, and having the forks resprung and valved at Traxxion.

Max's 900RR Answer

The symptom of a bike wanting to stand up in a turn comes from having *way* too soft fork springs, as is the case with most stock fork springs. In this case, the bike was actually riding through the turn with the fork bottomed out. Since there is no suspension travel left to absorb the centripetal force of the bike turning, it tries to do the only thing it can, which is roll over to the outside of the turn, or stand up. This went away when you applied lots of throttle, because you made the forks extend and gave them available travel again.

2000 Honda RC51

Kent: The RC51 lost traction at the front during turn-in. Not enough front weight bias? Lowering the front and raising the rear gave me my desired turn-in feel.

The 160-pound rider who purchased Kent's SV650 is contributing author Pat Hahn pictured here on the Suzuki at Brainerd International Raceway. Jonah K./Momentum Photo

Max: What do you mean "lost traction"? Did you lower the front and raise the rear at the same time? You would not know which cured the problem.

Kent: Lost traction: If I didn't get on the gas during turn-in, the front wheel would push. I like to brake and turn while letting off the brakes. I like to complete the turn-in flick so I reach full lean and hit my knee slider at the same time I finish getting completely off the brakes and not yet on the gas. The feel I like is a loaded front that bites and squirms under the load. Normally, it's as soon as I feel the full-load bite that I start to roll on the gas and pull weight off the front tire.

The RC51 would never give me that full-load bite I like. As I turned in and got off the brakes, I got nothing from the front. It felt like it would just continue to slide to the outside. The only way I could get the front to feel like it would turn was to catch it with the throttle as I turned in. I couldn't wait for the turn to finish and get the bite I like; I had to get on the gas to "wheelie" the front end around the corner.

This problem went away when I raised the back and lowered the front at the same time. I got back the feel I like, but it's true I don't know which cured the problem.

Max: I'm having trouble with this. The two "fixes" you mention contradict each other. Lowering the front and raising the rear will put more weight on the front end. Getting on the gas will take weight off the front. Your riding change directly contradicts your geometry change. Did you change anything else? You had an all-stock bike; you just changed geometry? How much did you change each end of the bike?

Kent: I dropped the triple down the forks another two lines or about 10 mm. I put three washers on top of the shock at the top shock mount. The washers were about 2 mm each for a total of 6 mm. That got the back end up about 2 inches.

Note that the riding "fix" didn't give me the front-end bite I wanted. It just allowed me to turn the corner without the front end sliding. I still never felt like the front was getting a firm contact with the pavement. I got the feel I was looking for only after the geometry change.

Max: Well, putting in the washers didn't get you 2 inches. The RC51 has about a 3 to 1 ratio of ride height to shock length. Adding 6 mm to the shock length would get you about 18 mm of ride height. That's less than 3/4 of an inch. Still, why would getting on the gas during drop-in stop the push? Hey! The RC51 doesn't have a slipper clutch, right?

Kent: Nope. It's a stock 2000 model.

Max's RC51 Answer

NOW I GOT IT! The RC51 has tons of engine braking and no slipper clutch. When you shut off the gas on a big twin, the engine braking makes the rear suspension want to collapse. This unloads the front tire, and makes it seem disconnected from the ground. By opening the throttle, you were able to take away the collapsing force on the rear suspension, and the bike returned to a more neutral attitude, and would then have more front bite. By lowering the front and raising the rear of the bike, the more aggressive attitude on the chassis makes it so the front wheel always has more of a dynamics load, even under engine braking.

2002 Suzuki SV650

Kent: The SV650 pushed mid-turn, just after coming back on the throttle. Perhaps that's a too-soft spring that lets the forks bottom?

Max: Where was your rear ride height set at? What tires were you using? What spring had we put on the shock? When you say "push," would the front feel disconnected from the ground, or would the bike run wide at the exit of the turn, or both?

Your comment about letting "forks bottom" is lost. I don't know where you got that. Once you open the throttle, the forks are not going to be bottomed out no matter what.

Kent: The rear ride height was whatever you get when you fit the standard Penske. Tires were Michelin Pilot Race M2/S2. Spring was set for a 180-pound rider and I was 205 pounds at the

time. Mid-turn, when on the gas, felt like the front wasn't going to hold. It didn't feel like it was going to tuck; it felt more like it was floating and losing traction because it was losing contact with the ground. I could get the bike to follow my desired line only by going slower or by spinning up the rear so it was pivoting faster than the front was pushing.

Tom Mason, my trusted tire guy, suggested that I may be bottoming out the forks. Seeing as I was 25 pounds heavier than the 180 pounds I asked you to set up the forks for, I thought that it may make sense. I never checked because I liked riding with the rear end sliding. It was fun! Well, until I crashed.

Max's SV650 Answer

Several things are possible causes of this problem. In the fork, it could be not enough free sag, or too slow of rebound damping. Either of these things makes it so the wheel doesn't want to drop out and stay in contact with the ground when the front end is light under acceleration. With the shock, too soft of a spring and/or too low of a rear ride height are likely the causes. It is most likely that the bike was squatting under acceleration, and taking away the dynamic load on the front tire. In particular, Michelin tires have much different geometry than Dunlops or Pirellis. Their rear tire has a much smaller diameter, and their front tire has a much larger diameter. This would make the bike more chopper-like and require a much more dramatic geometry setup.

Contact Information
Max McAllister
    President
    Traxxion Dynamics, Inc.
    261 Rope Mill Parkway, #3
    Woodstock, GA 30188

    (770) 592-3823 Office
    (770) 517-9332 Fax
    www.traxxion.com
    info@traxxion.com

CHAPTER FIVE

THE MEAT AND POTATOES

So you have prepared yourself and your bike and it's time to hit the track. There's a good deal to know before you go out there and flog it. You need to know what you're getting into. You need to know what to expect. You need to know what is expected of you. You need to know some basics. And you need to have a backup plan.

How much is it worth to have the undivided attention of three-time world champion Fast Freddie Spencer? Sign up to spend time with Freddie at www.fastfreddie.com. Kent Larson

As you move through the spectrum of less-controlled track events to more-controlled track events, you're making a tradeoff—you're giving up some freedom to do what you want to do, and exchanging it for added margins of safety and, more important, quality feedback from control riders and instructors.

The easiest way to measure what you're getting is by price. The more control and instruction, generally, the higher the price. The less the entry fee—again, generally—the less service you'll get. (However, the opposite is not always true. If you pay a premium price, you may not receive terrific service! On my first track day, it cost me an extra $70 to learn absolutely nothing from two well-meaning but otherwise useless instructors.) It's up to you to choose which is the track event for you. Do you want to learn on your own and have everyone else just do their own thing, or do you want to take the time to listen and learn from someone who knows and has already been there? Are you willing to spend the money to learn from someone like Keith Code or Freddie Spencer, or do you want to pay the minimum and get out there and just turn some laps? If you're concerned with your safety as well as learning some new tricks, do you want to attend a wide-open, 3 p.m.-until-dusk track day for $60 along with every other squid in the five-state region, or do you want to do a two-day learning center with an accomplished road racer for $2,265 and get some serious one-on-one instructor time?

The open and controlled track events generally allow you to ride your own pace and style, leaving much of the learning up to you. Nearly every track organization breaks up riders into groups according to either speed or experience, so you'll only rarely be stuck in a group that doesn't ride at a pace similar to yours.

The track schools and race schools have a definite agenda. You'll be ponying up your dough to learn what they want you to learn. On the other hand, the less-controlled schools also, by definition, have less control over individual riders and safety, whereas

At the more structured, controlled track day events such as the Northeast Sportbike Association (www.nesba.com) one-on-one attention is readily available. If you aren't getting the help you need, just ask. Jarel Jenson

Sportbike Track Time (www.sportbiketracktime.com) is one of the many organizations to choose from. Jack Beaudry

the more-controlled events take safety and rules—and outcomes—very seriously. Essentially, what you give up in freedom and self-education you balance out with safety and instruction. The best way to measure this is with price. Like riding gear, you generally get what you pay for.

Which Way Is the Right Way?

Track day organizations will always teach you the "right" way to ride. However, you will never come away from one of those events having learned the "right" way. Neither will you come away from one of those events having learned the "wrong" way. You will have learned what the organizers of those events believes is the best way (or the way to the quickest results!)

This is why the free world is really great: there are scores of different organizations from which to choose for track time, and they each have a different idea of what it means to ride on a track, and different ideas of what they want to accomplish. Track days, and the thrill of riding and riding fast, can be had over and over again, in many different ways, on different bikes using different approaches to riding, each one slightly different than the last, trying new combinations until you find what really floats your boat.

Types of Track Days

Open track days
In a nutshell, you're responsible for yourself and they're just giving you a cheap way to get your rocks off in a relatively safe place. This is most like riding in the real world, except you're in a safer environment than the street. These organizations believe that riding your own ride, at your own pace, and learning exactly what you want to learn is the priority. They also don't worry too much about interaction between faster, experienced riders and newbies. After all, that happens on the street every day, so what's wrong with letting it happen in a safer environment where you can learn to deal with it?

Controlled track days
Basically, you're still responsible for yourself and you get cheap thrills, but you also have some discipline—exactly what real, safe riding is all about. It's okay to hang it all out as long as you know what you're doing and you keep it within certain boundaries. To get the most out of a controlled track event, you absolutely must be able to admit that you might not know everything there is to

know about riding. You must also be able to follow rules. You don't have to like them, but you have to respect them for the sake of your co-riders.

Schools

Now you've accepted that there's something you can learn from someone else, especially someone faster than you. You'll have a choice of who you want to learn from, but you have to suspend everything you know for the purpose of the school, because for that day/weekend/week, you're going to learn it *their* way. It's okay to immerse yourself into a new riding style, even if only for a weekend, because you'll be able to compare it to your own riding style—and other riding styles—for the rest of your life, and continue to learn from it.

Two professional racers (Eric Bostrom in green and Larry Pegram in red) show very different riding styles. They both have successful racing careers. Is one riding more "right" than the other? Kent Larson

Race schools

Here you're dedicated and you have very little choice about what you learn. You either learn it or you don't get to race. However, you still have a lot of freedom regarding how you ride. Race schools really appreciate that everyone has a different riding style and they respect individuals' choices of bikes, gear, strategy, and positioning. They don't care if your technique is different from theirs. That's what makes racing interesting, anyway. Their job is to teach you the rules and give you some basic track and racing techniques, plus a lot of business about safety. This is a good thing—while you're out there racing, you want to be damned sure that everyone else on the track knows what you know, and follows the same rules you do.

However, just because it's for a race license doesn't mean the other riders actually know what they're doing. Remember, any idiot with a bike and a few hundred bucks can get a race certification. I saw a newbie have an idiot moment at Mid-America Motorplex and take out three gridded riders. This genius thought the green flag for the warm-up lap meant the race was actually on, and plowed into the back of the grid at 60 mph.

While you may not learn much other than commonsense items from most of these schools, you'll come away (assuming you survive the new rider race intact) with something you can't get from any of the other schools: a license to compete with other riders on the racetrack.

No Matter What

No matter what the organization is trying to teach you, there are some basic rules you should adhere to, to protect yourself and to promote your own evolution as a rider.

Take care

Use the same precautions you would on the street. You're still responsible for your own safety and knowing your own limits, and the track has a whole different angle of hazards and hazardous situations. Instead of being faced with a light changing from red to yellow when there's a car waiting to turn into the intersection and a Canyonero Intimida SUV riding your rear on a suburban arterial, you have to decide whether to share the corner with a rider who dropped in on you after you'd thrown it in, or to stand the bike up and run off the track and hope to stop before you plow into the bleachers. Either way, crashing hurts, so use your head.

Once you have your amateur license and some yellow number plates, you are ready to start racing. For someone with the right personality, this is much, much more fun than open track time. Jack Beaudry

Some people say riding on the track is safer than riding on the street. This would be true only if everyone rode at street speeds while on the track. What you gain in lack of hazards and surprises on the track, you trade off for increased speed and commitment to the quality of your tires and suspension. Don't go crazy out there just because there's no speed limit.

I have a good friend, Ray, who is one of the smoothest, fastest street riders whom I know. I'm constantly trying to get him to a track day so we can ride together in a "safer" environment. I can ride with him on the street, but he puts down a pace that is on the ragged edge of my comfort zone for street riding. So, come on, Ray, let's go to Road America and see what these machines can really do.

Ray would always refuse. When I pressed him to explain, he admitted that he didn't trust himself. On the street, the added dangers and unknowns force you to hold back a bit. Nobody is going to ride at ten-tenths for long on the street. If anyone is faster than you on the street, it can be shrugged off as just some fool willing to ride the road with less reserve.

At the track, you can push it to the limit and ride with little or no reserve. That's even expected behavior to many riders. If someone is faster than you at the track, that just makes him or her "better" than you. You can't use the holding-back-for-safety excuse. Holding back just means that you aren't in complete control of your bike. If you are in complete control, you can ride at the bike's limit, not at the edge of your comfort zone.

Ray feels his competitive nature would not allow him to stay within his comfort zone. On the track, he feels a faster rider would prompt him to ride faster than he would like. I think just the fact he is concerned about control of his competitiveness puts him on the safe end of the risks verses rewards scale. Someone willing to admit that ego may be a problem is much more able to check it at the door. Most every track school gives the check-your-ego-at-the-door speech before riding starts. Those who can actually follow that advice learn the most and improve the fastest.

On the street, the largest component of the risk you face is determined by the operators of other vehicles and surprises from the surrounding environment. On the track, the largest risk component is the operator of your motorcycle. It's up to you to determine how fast you go and the risks you take. If you can't trust yourself, you should stay off the track. I have to respect Ray's assessment but I'll continue to work on him. I'm confident he would do just fine. By staying off the track, he is missing one of the most satisfying experiences he can have with his bike.

Ride your own ride

Just because you all line up at pit zero and descend en masse to the track surface doesn't mean that you don't have a mind of your own. I promise you, for every one

At Blackhawk Farms Raceway, the beginner and intro group get a track walk and instruction during a NESBA day. Jack Beaudry

rider on the track who knows what he or she is doing, there is at least one rider out there who doesn't. (That type of rider, typically on a 600- or 1000-cc sportbike, is especially fun to pass on a ratty old GS 500.) Those riders just want to go fast and have fun, and really have no idea how to control a bike. It's important to ignore what everyone else is doing and focus on you, your bike, and the track.

Just as on the street, on the track there are a hundred different lane positions and speeds from which to choose. Do what makes the most sense for you and your riding style (allowing for the track/organization rules, of course). Don't fall into the trap of zoning in on another rider's tail section. This is as easy and dangerous as target fixating on off-track objects. If you spend too much time watching the rider in front of you for your cues, when that rider makes a mistake he or she automatically makes that mistake for you, too—and mistakes are costly out there.

Watch out for the other guy

Events that are open to the unlicensed public can be just as chancy as riding on the street—there is the same ratio of idiots on the track as there are in the real world. For example, for every nine car drivers that drive predictably and safely, there is at least one who has no real clue what's going on out there, or how much danger they're putting everyone else in. You have that same one-

in-ten ratio on the track, as well. Trust your instinct and steer clear of anyone who gives you the willies. Your instinct is probably correct, and there's usually a good reason to avoid that person.

Until you're ready to start dicing it up and trading paint with other riders, steer clear of crowds. If you find yourself constantly tailgating a group of squids who can go fast as hell on the straights and then throw anchors out in the corners, pull off on the next lap and count to thirty. Take a few deep breaths. Forget them. Concentrate on yourself. You'll be calmer and more collected for it, and you'll give the socialites a chance to get far enough ahead of you so that you can do your own thing again. Passing on the track takes planning and finesse; don't jump into it before you're ready to accept the risks.

Keep in mind that you are always going to encounter idiots any time you interact with others. Everyone is an idiot some of the time, including you and me. Everyone in the world has occasionally done something followed immediately by the crystalline insight of "oh, *that* was stupid." For some, it's the last thought they have. For others, the realization serves as training that lowers their Idiot Percentage (IP).

As I said earlier, your IP is the percentage of time you spend being an idiot. If you were a complete idiot, your IP would be 100. I hope the people you spend time with on the racetrack will have IPs below, say, one-eighth. But even then you never know if you

Karl Rehpohl (No. 80) and Dr. Dave Johnson (No. 242) share the corner at Brainerd International Raceway, turn 10. Tony Marx

are going to be right there when that IP=0.00000001 individual is having an "oh, *that* was stupid" Idiot Moment.

For example, there's this racer with the CRA that I'll call "Calvin." I ran into Calvin at Brainerd International Raceway back in 2001. Actually, it's more accurate to say he ran into me.

I was using the Central Roadracing Association's Friday all-day practice to feel out new tires and my recently repaired R6. I hit the track for the first time right after lunch and timed it so I entered just after the only other bikes running had passed track out. There were only a few riders ready to jump out just after lunch so I'd get a couple lonely laps to see how the bike and I were recovering from my own Idiot Moment (IM) at Daytona that spring.

Got up to speed in turn 1, took turns 2, 3, and 4 at about three-quarter speed and was drifting out to set up turn 5 when *wham!* I'm on the ground. I thought I was all alone (IM for me) but Calvin had followed me out. He was attempting to make an outside pass at the entrance to turn 5 and ran out of track as I drifted wide to hit my turn-in point.

Now, I'm not going to call Calvin a complete idiot. That would be slanderous. I'm sure there are some times when Calvin is not having an Idiot Moment, but I don't really hang out with him so I haven't seen any. My only interaction was during his enormous Idiot Moment when he decided to break my ankle with his front tire instead of moving to the inside or taking to the grass.

Let me reiterate what I feel is the most important rule when it comes to riding with other bikes: It is the rider doing the passing who is responsible for making the pass safe. This applies to racing, track day riding, or riding on the street. If you are the bike in the back, it is your job to make sure you don't hit the bike you are following or attempting to pass. No matter how stupid a move the other bike makes, if you hit it from behind, it is your fault! No questions.

Don't think that there's an ongoing feud between me and Calvin. He admitted his fault and said he was sorry at the time. Later, he wanted to blame me. "You took the whole track away from me by running all the way to the outside!" But I know that's just so he can feel better about himself. Too late, Calvin, I've already forgiven you.

Racing and track days are a lot more dangerous than sitting on your couch watching TV. If you do it long enough, you will eventually be caught up in an incident. No matter what happens, try to adopt the philosophy that it is your fault for being there. It took me three months to recover physically and three years to recover mentally from my incident with Calvin. I wanted to blame him and be mad at him for breaking my foot; costing me a helmet, leathers, and a set of bodywork; and ruining my racing season. I finally realized it wasn't his fault; it was mine. I chose to be out on the track that day. Just my deciding to be there puts the blame on me no matter how stupid someone else was during an incident.

Clayton Tutor is really just playing for the camera here and isn't about to be high-sided into the air fence. Jim Lilly

Try to adopt this philosophy and you will save yourself a lot of stress. Calvin pissed me off for years. Not because of anything he was doing—the incident was over a long time ago for him—but because of what I was doing by holding on to my anger. All I had to do was let go and the incident was over for me too. Always be ready to forgive and forget. Always blame yourself; you made the choice to interact with other idiots while playing a high-risk sport. Make sure you are comfortable with the risk verses rewards analysis before you go out on track for the first time.

Since the incident with Calvin, I've resolved to never be at less than full speed when on the track. At full speed, people don't pass you, you pass them. When you are doing the passing, you have the control. You decide when the pass is safe. If you made a bad decision, you can abort the attempt and prevent an Idiot Moment that takes out another rider.

It takes a fairly low IP to run a fast lap time. The high IP riders either need to go slow enough to recover from their many Idiot Moments Per Lap (IMPL) or they crash. IMPL of 1 or higher is going to put you in the crash truck before too long. Either way, they aren't going to catch you. If you are running full out fast laps, after one lap, only a low IP rider is going to catch you. If you are being passed, you have a much better chance of avoiding someone else's Idiot Moment if you are getting passed by another low IP rider. At the same time, fast laps give you the luxury of doing a quick IP analysis on the riders you are catching before you attempt a pass on them.

If you can't do lap times consistently faster than most of the group you ride with, don't go to open, uncontrolled track events. Stick to the structured and passing rule loaded organizations such as the Northeast Sportbike Association (www.nesba.com). If you can't stay away from the idiots out there, you should at least stay where the idiots are not allowed to run free.

Be consistent

Riding at a higher level requires a good bit of trust in the other riders. Just as the corners become predictable as you do them over and over again, riders on the track should become predictable as well. Don't suddenly change your game plan in the middle of a corner. Everyone has a different riding style, and you'll encounter 20 to 40 different riding styles every time you hit the track. It's okay to have a different style, but it's not okay to change that style willy-nilly. Even though you don't have any turn signals or brake lights on the track, it's still a good idea to give others an idea of what you're going to do. You do that by remaining consistent with your speed and lines. If you make changes, make them *gradually*. Remember: those other riders are trying to negotiate

Monte Lutz and Bonnie Strawser from Sportbike Track Time (www.sportbike-tracktime.com) are two riders with way more than enough track time to get smooth with the controls. Thanks to the efforts of Monte, Bonnie, and the many other track day organizers, you too can enjoy as much track time as you want. Jack Beaudry

the same track. They are going just as fast, and they are also probably experimenting and learning. They may not be ready for any surprises. Just as on the street, surprises are generally bad things.

Be smooth: acceleration, braking, cornering, transitions

I have never seen a jerky, ham-fisted rider ride fast or well. However, all accomplished riders, whether on the track or on the street, are all as smooth as glass in every move they make. They're fluid. Being smooth is the foundation for ten-tenths riding. If you're not smooth from the very outset, everything you do will be tainted by what you cannot do. You can master the skill of hanging off the bike, but if you're fumbling with the brakes or throttle or handlebars, you'll look like a monkey at a typewriter—at 80 mph. Take the time to get the basic skill of smoothness ironed out first. At a track day, a smooth rider on a 500 will smoke a jerky rider on a liter bike any day.

Riding smoothly will make it possible for you to ride far better and faster than any other new skills you acquire. Late braking, combining braking and cornering, flicking the bike in, hard acceleration, lighting up, and sliding the tires are all skills that could reduce your lap times, but none are as important or have as big an impact as being smooth. I once spent half a track day nearly crashing in every corner, running wide, making mistakes, and feeling like

someone else's hands were attached to my arms and someone else's brain was telling them what to do. Then I realized I was trying to go fast, and I forgot to keep it smooth. In the very next session, not only did I feel more comfortable out there, my lap times dropped as well.

One way to look at your goal of smooth riding is to make it difficult for an observer on the sidelines to see you brake (squeeze the lever/press the pedal, compress forks), accelerate (twist the throttle, flatten the rear, lighten the front wheel), start your turn-in (press the bars, lean your body in), or start your drive out of the corners (tuck back in and twist the throttle). You should strive to make it look like a magic trick: Look, Ma! No transitions!

Take your time

It takes a few sessions to learn the facility before you start experimenting. Build up to new skills and boundaries gradually. Your ability to ride well has much to do with your state of mind and degree of focus. It takes time to warm up to the point where you're ready to do some ten-tenths riding. Just because you may have done it a month ago doesn't mean you're ready to do it again at a moment's notice. Why do you suppose so many crashes happen in the first lap of a race?

Of course you'll need to take it easy first thing in the morning when the track, your tires, and your muscles are cool and rested. But also pay particular attention to your mindset after a longer-than-normal break, such as a lunch break or a red-flag delay. Too much cool-down time means you'll need more warm-up time when you get back out there. Don't just go from ice cold to red hot without some transition time, and use extra caution until you're back in the game. These rules apply to street riding too. Ever been on an uneventful group ride, then stopped for lunch, and ten minutes after getting back on the bikes, someone crashes? That rider just jumped back in where he or she left off, instead of warming up.

Relax

Stay in control of your mind, your emotions, your body, and your machine. Being tense, full of adrenaline, or afraid will make you do things you wish you hadn't. Be calm and certain of the limits of your skills, your bike, your environment, and your goals. If you're out there learning too much or pushing too hard, and things are coming at you rapid-fire and your mind goes into mental overload, dial it back a notch or pit out for the rest of that session until you regain your composure. Concentration is everything at track speeds. If you don't have it, find a chair and a cold glass of water and collect yourself. Good rule of thumb: if you nearly soil your leathers more than once in a session, get off the track. Take a break. It could be just a visit to the restroom, or it could be that you're about one slight mistake away from a crash.

Build up gradually

Don't go out there and try to master everything you've read about and learned all at once. Start with your basic street skills and

How much would using the back brake help here? This shouldn't be happening on the track. If you constantly loft the rear wheel, you either have a suspension problem (forks are bottoming) or you are stabbing at the front brake lever instead of being smooth. Vern Nichols

work up one skill at a time. Don't expect to get it all in one day. Can you imagine trying to learn to play the piano and expecting to jump to master-pianist level with a few lessons and a day of dedicated practice? No way. Any good rider will tell you they learn something new every time they ride. The same goes for the track. But if you try to do too many new things too quickly, you'll overheat your brain and lose it all, which could put you at risk out there. Better to build up a little at a time.

The great thing about track riding is predictability—every corner is the same, every time. Once you get used to the track, it frees up a little bit of your mind to add additional tasks to your brain—to learn, to experiment, and to get better. You have to make room if you want to add more. You can pack more in by adding skills gradually.

Know your limits

It is absolutely critical that you know the limits of your mind and your body—and always remain within those limits. What keeps you from fragging your bike on the track and landing you in an

ambulance is your brain, and the appendages that your brain relies on to control the bike. Take careful note of your fatigue and attention level. If you were up late the night before, you may not be able to perform as well as you would otherwise, and you may need to back off or skip a few sessions. Be aware of any distractions (mental, emotional, physical) that could interfere with your perception and the free flow of information and electrical signals from your brain to your hands and feet. Eat healthy foods and drink lots of water and juice. And pay attention to your body. If you become tired, sore, overheated, chilly, or even dizzy or nauseous, it's time to call it quits, at least for a while. Riding on the track can take a terrific amount of physical effort, especially for the newer track rider. Unless you're relatively fit, you'll wear out your body a lot quicker than you expect. Don't let your mind or body become exhausted while you're out there shredding apexes.

The hydration issue deserves a bit more attention than just "drink plenty of water." You hear that all the time. Your parents, coach, spouse, and local weathermen are always harping "be

Looking well up the track keeps your attention focused on where you are going, not where you are. By the time you reach your turn-in point, you should be looking at the apex. By the time you reach the apex, you should be looking at the corner exit. Jack Beaudry

sure to drink a lot. . . ." Yeah, yeah, yeah, *what*ever. I'm an active guy. I know my limits. Shut up already.

No, listen. Really! Pay attention. When you are on the track on a hot day you dehydrate faster than you think. Sweat is poring out of you and you probably don't even notice it evaporating as fast as it is produced. (You did buy a fully perforated set of full leathers like Jason Bishop recommends, right?) Frequently, the only evidence of sweating is the strange white stains left on your shirt and the fact that you've been drinking all day but haven't had to pee once.

I down at least 20 ounces of fluid every hour when I'm at the track. I make sure I have access to a trackside refrigerator and freezer (by bringing them with me in my travel trailer). What works well for me is to put a water bottle or sports drink in the freezer. When I come off the track I replace the one in the freezer with another from the fridge and enjoy a semi-frozen refreshment while I relax and talk to my buds. Every time I come in, there's a cold-cold-cold drink ready for me.

Be sure to avoid caffeinated beverages. You may think you are satisfying your thirst but these drinks actually take more water out of your body than they put in. At least that's what we always hear so it must be true, right? I'm not a doctor or biologist and I don't really know how that works. Study that on your own if you like; I'll just believe the experts who keep repeating that warning.

Do, however, alternate between water and sports drinks designed to replace lost electrolytes. Remember those strange white stains on your cloths? That's the salt left behind when your sweat evaporated. If you don't replace the lost salt, your body's pH balance will get screwed up and cause problems.

Don't screw around. Bring lots of fluids and drink often. Bring some to share and force it on your buddies every time you are relaxing between track sessions. Not following this advice can be fatal. Minnesota Vikings Korey Stringer died from pushing too hard and not drinking enough. I spent the last two laps of a GTU race at Topeka, Kansas, trying to not pass out because I was dehydrated.

Videographer Michael Casey at work. Can you pick out the camera over the middle 4 on the 447 bike? If you are going to hire someone to follow you and produce a video of your riding, be sure to get someone who can keep up.
Jack Beaudry

After the race, it took me six hours of air-conditioned relaxation and constant downing of sport drinks before I started to feel normal.

Remember the Basics

Remember the basics of motorcycle riding on the street, because they are the base foundation for track riding: braking, looking through the turn, countersteering, and space cushioning. Don't start adding weapons to your riding arsenal until you're mastered these, first—know thyself. If you aren't positive that you're 100 percent capable of the four basic skills below, don't take on any additional information. If need be, ignore the instructors and practice these things until they're solid.

Braking:

Braking should be done smoothly, with both brakes simultaneously, and should be completed before the start of the turn. If you are the least bit fearful of using your front brake, you have to learn. On the track, the front brake is responsible for 90 to 100 percent of your stopping ability.

Many racers insist that they don't use the back brake at all and watching almost any race will show examples where the back tire is off the ground during braking. If you consistently lift the back wheel while braking properly, there really isn't a need to be using the back brake. However, even the most advanced rider usually only lifts the back tire because they were a bit too grabby and stabbed at the front brake. Until you are hauling your bike down from speed with the back wheel balanced just at the limit of contact, you have reason to be using both brakes. Any less braking from the front will give you traction at the rear wheel that can be used to help slow the bike.

Some riders/racers dispense with rear braking just so they don't have yet another thing to think about while riding. Since proper application of the front brake greatly reduces the effectiveness of braking with the almost weightless back wheel, these

The Pat-n-Tommy video team may be good enough for your first track day but expect to soon be leaving them behind. Chris Ellickson

concentration farther ahead, you get the feeling that everything is slowing down which, in turn, allows you to go faster.

Countersteering:

Your grasp of the concept and application of countersteering needs to be firm. Some people will tell you that it's your body that does most of the steering, but unless you're a world-class road racer, you're not ready yet to rely on your body positioning alone. Use the handlebars to flick the bike into turns, turning the bars to the left to throw it into a right hander, and turning the bars to the right to throw it into a left hander. If you don't know how to do this yet, stay off the track. Heck, stay off the street until you can get some basic training.

Even good riders who understand the countersteering concept will frequently exhibit a common problem of fighting with themselves. That is, they use both arms to steer rather then simply pushing on the inside bar, or the bar that is on the same side of the bike that the rider intends to turn. When they use both arms, the arm on the outside of the turn is simply fighting the arm on the inside of the turn.

I once had a pretty fast rider come up and ask me how much pressure it took to hold a bike down in a corner. I said "Huh?" He said "You know, when you are mid-corner, how much force are you using on the bars to keep the bike turning." My answer was: "Well, none actually. If it were possible to lock the throttle open so I didn't have to hold the right bar, I could stay in a corner without touching either bar." I frequently run laps one-handed when I'm doing the Control Rider gig with NESBA and even when steering with just my right arm all day, it's not my arm that is tired at the day's end.

In his book *Total Control*, Lee Parks talks about a great teaching concept he uses. He instructs the rider to use only one arm at a time for steering inputs. Try this sometime. When turning right, only use the right arm to push on the bar. Make sure your left arm is totally relaxed during right-hand turns. When going left, only use the left arm and focus on using nothing from the right arm except throttle control. After trying this, students who showed the symptoms of fighting among themselves are always floored by how easy it is to turn. A brilliantly simple exercise that very clearly shows riders how much improper steering input they have been applying for years.

riders are not giving up much. It may well be worth the braking loss to reduce the mental clutter.

Looking through the turn:

Visual directional control, a.k.a. looking through the turn, is the centerpiece around which all high-performance riding revolves. If you're not comfortable looking at least two to four seconds ahead of you (at any speed!), you need to sort that out before you move on to any advanced techniques. If you start to get a speed rush panic when on the track, take notice of where you are looking. Looking down at the track just in front of your bike makes it seem like everything is happening way too fast. By the time you react to what you are seeing, it's already upon you. Slow down a tad and start extending your view. The farther down the track you look, the more time you have to react to what's coming. By extending your

Doing the shadow thing at a NESBA track day. Jack Beaudry

Needing steering pressure on the bars mid-corner and wearing out your upper body instead of your lower body are the classic symptoms of this bad behavior.

Space cushions:

Finally, remember space cushioning, both in your relationship to the track and to the other riders. Just as proper positioning and personal space keep you alive in real-world traffic, they're imperative to staying safe on the track. Don't put yourself into a position in which you have no way out. Keep your options open by giving yourself a constant cushion of time and space to do your thing. Just because you saw Valentino Rossi bump up against Max Biaggi in a MotoGP race doesn't mean it's a good idea for you to do the same. Remember, Rossi and Biaggi are paid millions of dollars per year to race for world championships; you are just having fun at a track day.

These are the basic things that keep you safe on the street; use them to keep you rubber side down on the track. If you aren't completely comfortable with these techniques and able to do them without even thinking, concentrate on those things only and don't worry about what the organizers are trying to teach you. Adding additional tasks to a mind that is overtaxed already is asking—no, it's begging—for a crash. It's okay to go to a track day without knowing the basics, as long as that's what you practice while you're out there. They'll reward you with big payoffs in safety and control, both on the track and on the street, and will provide a solid foundation upon which to build race skills at future track days.

Be Humble and Open-Minded

Get used to the idea that there may be some things about riding you don't know yet. Get used to the thought of trying high-level riding techniques. And be prepared to try some things that don't make sense at first, things that may seem counterintuitive, or things that may just seem plain crazy. The laws that apply to street riding can be bent for the purposes of track riding. You'll try faster approaches and charge into corners like you never thought possible. You'll try your hand at late braking. You may experiment with trail braking, and combining braking with turning instead of separating them like you do on the street. You'll learn to toss the bike into turns, quickly and decisively,

When learning to hang off, work on the upper body first. Get used to having the throttle right in the middle of your chest when going right and way over there on the other side of the bike when going left. Don't even think about lower body movement until you are comfortable with your upper body movement shifting all the controls on you. Don't get stuck on top of your bike like this rider.
Jack Beaudry

rather than wasting time at a lean angle that doesn't pull you through the corner.

Of course, you'll have to get used to 100 percent acceleration, 100 percent braking, and 100 percent cornering and lean angles. This is ten-tenths riding. And you'll do it all in tight traffic—there could be 20 to 40 other riders out there on the track with you, some riding at your level and learning the same things you're learning. Some will be just beginning their track adventure and holding you up in the corners. Still others who have mastered the track will be looking to improve their lap times while you are just in the way.

Lap Timers

One way to measure your riding improvement is in your lap times. Consider investing in a lap timer, renting one at the track, or having a friend time your laps while you're out there. Getting consistent lap time readings can help you analyze your skill development and whether or not your latest "trick" helps or hurts your overall speed, but it can also shoot you warning signs: if your lap

times suddenly drop and you smell oil, or if your lap times become erratic and you're feeling really thirsty, you have an advance notice of something else that might be wrong.

Max McAllister points out lap times as a quick reality check on how well you have your suspension sorted. If you are riding the ragged edge barely in control of your slipping and bucking machine, but still can't get within five seconds of that other rider on the same stock equipment, then either you suck or your bike sucks. If you feel pretty confident you are riding smooth and well but limited by the bike, then you have evidence that your suspension may need some work.

Try a Photographer

Another way to analyze your performance is to view it after the fact. Consider having a photographer (or videographer) keep track of you throughout the day. If you were having trouble with a certain turn or section of the track, some audio/visual aids may help you discern what was missing from your riding style. Many tracks have photographers who earn their living shooting track days. Ask around and let that photographer know you'd like to buy some photos, and which turns you'd most like to see. If no photographer is available, bring a friend and offer them free sunscreen, beer, and food to spend the day taking pictures of you.

Jack Beaudry of SliderPhoto.com (www.sliderphoto.com) is one of the best and most active trackside photographers in the business. If you want some good shots of yourself railing a corner, go on the SliderPhoto website and get to an event Jack is going to cover. After a pre-ride talk with Jack, you could leave with 27 eight-by-ten color glossy pictures with circles and arrows and a paragraph on the back of each one or—if you would rather—a CD full of digital shots. Even without the pre-ride talk, Jack will probably have a dozen quality photos of you but, if you know you want to buy some pictures, talking to Jack first will help make sure you have plenty from which to choose.

Be sure to do a quality check before dropping cash on a photographer. Any work I've gotten from Jack Beaudry has been worth far more than what I've paid (but don't tell that to Jack). On the other hand, the hundred bucks I left with the substitute photographer working at a riding school put on by one of the greatest road racers in the history of the sport got me nothing more than seven useless, low-resolution digital photos that all

With enough open track time or track schools, your left turns can look as pretty as Ben Fruehauf's pictured here. As Ben puts it "Well, I ought to look good. What I've paid at track schools could put your daughter through college." Brad Schwab

looked about the same. Well, they are at least useful in showing that I'm pretty consistent through that particular turn.

The Power of Video

Michael J. Casey is running a new company, MotoVid.com (www.motovid.com), dedicated to providing video feedback to those who want it. This is an invaluable service for anyone interested in seeing what they are doing on the track. Having a DVD of yourself doing a few laps gives you a permanent record that can be used to impress your friends and family or solicit feedback from your favorite "expert."

MotoVid.com currently works most of the Midwest events with the Northeast Sportbike Association (www.nesba.com) and all the Midwest Learning Curves (www.learningcurves.com) outings. Check the MotoVid.com website for events near you.

Find a Shadow

Have an instructor, control rider, or riding buddy follow you for at least a couple of laps per session. While video or photographic feedback can help, nothing compares to hearing your story from someone else—especially someone who also knows how to ride and can speak our peculiar high-performance motorcycle language—to help you ride better. Remember to take it also with a grain of salt. What works for a regional club racing champ with 20 years of experience may not work for you.

Beware of JTL

You never, ever want to find yourself out there "Just Turning Laps." A hamster in a wheel is just turning laps. A jogger on a treadmill is just turning laps. If you're not making discoveries out there, leave the bike parked until you start learning something or working on a particular technique or corner. (One of Keith Code's rules in the California Superbike School is, "You must improve.") Riding, even on a track, is too risky to be out there without any purpose or direction.

If you're not ready yet to try an instructor's riding style, you may want to devise your own instructional plan. Your goal should be to work on one thing at a time until your muscles memorize

If you're thinking about going racing but not quite sure you're ready, do some volunteer corner working. You can get up close to the action and see what's happening on the track during a race. By the end of the day, you'll know what to expect and can decide if you are ready to take the plunge. Tony Marx

what you're doing and you can start combining various riding skills into serious track techniques.

Included below are some sample track-riding drills to get you started, culled from the Enthusiastic Hedonism cornering seminars in the Minneapolis area. You probably won't be able to try them all in a day. You may have to spend several track days mastering them all. They're designed to be practiced in order, and the skills they develop go from simple to complex. Once you get into the more advanced techniques, it's okay to skip around a bit, but until you get comfortable with the first six drills, do them in order, even if it means doing them all over again at your next track day.

No matter how it works out, you could spend a whole summer of track days perfecting the techniques in these 10 sessions. Have fun with them. You may also wish to adapt them to the particular

school you're attending, or to your particular strengths and weaknesses. Remember: one new thing at a time. Don't cook your brain while you're hanging it out there at 100 mph.

Again, it must be stressed that this book is not trying to be a "how-to-ride" book. Please research and purchase a how-to book for more detailed direction. If you would rather get hands-on instruction, find a track school to give you direction. These exercises are just included to help until better instruction is acquired from a trusted track school or book.

Session 1: Track familiarization and sighting

Learn the track. Take it slow. Ride as if you're on the street. Scan every inch of the surface (it's okay to look at the ground during this session), assure yourself there's nothing to worry about. Memorize the corners: right, left, which gear they require, and their distance from the last corner. Find your lines.

Session 2: Sighting session and visual directional control

Learn the track more. Don't try too much yet. Now stick to two gears only (second/third or third/fourth), do not use your brakes at all, and concentrate on visual directional control (looking where you want to go) only. Keep your eyes off the ground, and focus on the track two to four seconds ahead of you and not the track just in front of your front tire. Find your markers for braking, turning in, and accelerating. Continue to find your lines. Watch what other riders choose for lines, as well.

Session 3: Countersteering

Again, use two gears only and no brakes as before, but this time, concentrate only on countersteering, using the handgrips to point the bike in the direction you want. Keep looking through the turns.

Session 4: Entry speed

Two gears only, but more acceleration, higher speed, and now really use your brakes to set your entry speed—the speed that allows you to roll on the throttle all the way through the turn. Try to stay on your lines. Add a little bit of speed at a time (not all at once), and note how your lines and position change depending on your use of the controls.

Session 5: Powerband

Use all your gears, but for now go back to no brakes again. Learn to keep the bike in the powerband at all times: straights, corner entry, apex, and exit. Use engine braking to slow you down. Get a feel for what gear the bike likes, and where.

Session 6: Altogether now

Combine all your gears with more acceleration on exits and straights and full braking to set up for corner entry. Now you're cooking with gas! Practice really getting on the throttle for the drive out of the corners, using the throttle to stand the bike up after the apex. Enjoy!

Session 7: Upper body English

You've probably gotten to the point where your lean angles are perilously close to scraping the ground with your footpegs or exhaust pipe. Now you're ready to try some body English. Learning to use your body is a big jump in riding evolution and uses up an enormous amount of concentration, so for this session, jump back three sessions to Session 4 and go back to using two gears, good acceleration, higher speeds, and braking to set entry speed—but now you're going to use your body to help the bike through the turn. Instead of leaning your body at the same angle of the bike, lean in with your head, shoulders, and torso, keeping a tight grip on the bike with your legs and knees and keeping your arms and elbows loose. Keep your speed down until you get a feel for hanging your body out there in the wind, but feel how much more stable your bike feels for the effort.

Session 8: Lower body English

Once you've gotten used to using your upper body to help corner the bike, it's time to get the lower body involved. Stay back in Session 4 like last time as you learn this. You're going to have to get your ass off the seat and your inside knee out in the breeze, while continuing to lean out with your upper body and grip the bike with your legs and knees and keep your shoulders, arms, and elbows relaxed. As always, add a little bit at a time. If you begin to feel mentally overloaded, back off and regroup, and try it again from a lower level of intensity.

Session 9: Total body English

Combine everything you've learned about using your body to help steer and control the bike, and combine it with Session 6. You're now just about in race form, working up to race pace, and the other riders are probably getting a look at your race face.

Session 10: Throw the bike into the turns

Now it's time to start really throwing the bike in. No dilly-dallying. Make your transition from straight up and down to full lean quick and decisive. Snap the bike over. Minimize the amount of time you spend leaning the bike, and try to give the bike only one steering input per corner. Approach, brake, body English, toss it in, apex, drive out, set up for the next—everything. Now you're ready to grind down those lap times!

You can try lots of things here, but overall, your priority is your own safety. Don't lose your mind and survival instinct just because there is no speed limit and no gravel in the corners. Keep your head and your wits about you, respect the cost of mistakes at ten-tenths, and get out there and have some fun.

CHAPTER SIX

MAKING THE LEAP FROM TRACK DAYS TO RACING

You should be warned that a motorcycle track day is a gateway drug. Some will build up a tolerance to the rush and need something more to be satisfied. This is the rider soon to be sucked into the life of a club racer.

Jason Bishop (foreground) and Tony Marx (background) and their Suzuki SV650 race bikes. Tony Marx

When you go on street rides, it's easy to identify an individual who is ripe for the addiction. It's the rider who always needs to be at the front or right on the rear wheel of the person leading the ride. You can tell that being considered the fastest is important. They may occasionally jump ahead of the route leader for short stints just to let everyone know the pace is a bit too boring for them.

In my efforts to recruit street riders to the track, I put these competitive bikers at the top of my hit list. The only way they are going to be satisfied is by racing other riders to prove their superiority by winning. Getting these riders to the track is the best thing that can happen to them. It's better for the image of our sport as well since getting these riders into racing helps reduce the number of crashes on public roads.

I could tell that I was one of these riders when I found myself dragging the fairings of my Honda ST1100 through nearly every turn at Deal's Gap just to show the rider following me with a Yamaha FZR that I could dust him. Things were working just fine until I realized this next turn was sharper than planned and I couldn't tighten up my line because I was already dragging hard parts. My competitive tendency put me in the ditch and I knew I needed to quit riding or go racing.

A few years ago, I noticed the telltale signs in a new friend, Jason Bishop. It wasn't because he rode over his head but because he had this intensity about him. He was always a proper and courteous rider, but he knew he was a winner and you could tell that he would prove it anytime needed. Jason was meant to race motorcycles, and I knew that getting him to a track day was all I needed to put him on the path.

Jason has had some trials and tragedies because of the addiction I helped cultivate. Sometimes I question if he would have been better off if I never tried to recruit him to the track. I

Two expert level club racers fighting it out at Brainerd International Raceway. White number plates are for experts. Yellow plates indicate a novice racer. Tony Marx

There is always the possibility that your race bike will end up as a smoking heap outside turn 10. You may want to start out racing on a bike that you are willing to see destroyed. Tony Marx

think not. Extreme riding is safest on the track. I firmly believe that even club racing is safer than riding your bike near its limit on the street. I could tell that if Jason didn't go racing, he was going to frequently find himself riding at the absolute limits on the street. If you, too, are highly competitive, you may find doing track days will soon lead to racing.

To help you through a possible track day to race day transition and to show what that jump could entail, I asked Jason to share his experience.

My Name Is Jason, and I'm a Motorcycle Road Racer

You just finished your first track day and there aren't enough words to describe what you're feeling right now. For most of you, it was without a doubt the most fun you've ever had on two wheels. You still can't believe how much fun you actually had tearing up that track. The level of fun varies from rider to rider, but there's a good chance that it may have been an experience that will change the way you look at motorcycles—and your disposable income—for the rest of your life.

I had about 13 years of street riding under my belt when I finally decided it was time to do my first track day. Actually I didn't really decide as much as I was bullied into it by a friend and mentor who saw something in me that I hadn't yet noticed. We'd done a couple of street rides together and hung out quite a bit, so my friend, the experienced control rider and road racer Kent Larson, kept pushing this track day stuff down my throat every chance he got. (I was riding a ZRX 1100 at the time and riding way too fast for the limitations of the street.) I resisted, and kept putting him off, saying that if I had a better bike I'd be all over it. Well, I changed my mind when a new track in Iowa opened up just a few hours away that offered cheap track days to get things going. Finally caving in, I jumped at the chance to get my feet wet.

You have probably had, or will have, a similar experience. Not quite confident to go it alone, you will convince a bunch of buddies to try a track day, too, and turn it into a weekend road trip. You'll spend the days and weeks beforehand talking about your upcoming track day, and you'll spend the entire car ride to the track pumping each other up. I think I got about three hours of

Finding sponsors can help offset the costs of racing. A contingency sponsor will pay you cash or product credit when you run their stickers and place in the top 3 or 5 or even sometimes in the top 10. Other sponsors may be willing to exchange cash or products just for running their stickers. Anyone racing can get contingency money by placing well enough. It's much harder to find a cash-up-front sponsor. Jason's race bike proudly displays his sponsors. Jonah K./Momentum Photo

sleep the night before my first track day. I was worried that my bike might not be good enough for something like this, and even more worried that my 13 years of riding on the street still hadn't prepared me for what I was getting into the next day. Turned out, I was right. And I was also wrong. But it took me a day at the track—several, actually—to learn exactly how I was right and wrong. In the meantime, the only comfort I had was knowing that a few of the guys out there with me the next day were friends in the exact same boat.

When the sun came up the morning of your first track day, you were probably already awake—stoked, tense—just laying in bed waiting for the alarm to go off and the gates at the track to open.

You arrived, checked in, and got all your bikes through tech inspection, sat fiddling with your gloves during the orientation, and then waited eagerly to hear them call your group over the loud speakers for the first session. Before you knew it, the control rider was leading you out onto the track and you were getting the first taste of true high-performance riding. Like me, you may have become frustrated right away, too.

I have to admit the first 20 minutes I spent on the track were kind of lame. I had signed up for the same beginner session as all my buddies, and we spent our first laps on the track in single file going agonizingly slow in order to get our bearings and learn the track. Even though I knew sighting laps were important, I wanted

Whenever you come off the pace, be sure to put up a hand or kick out your leg to let the other riders know you are now a slow moving object. Jack Beaudry

to go fast, damn it, and by the end of those 20 minutes I was so bored I was almost in tears. Let's twist the throttle already!

It probably happened the same way to you. And like my experience, yours probably got a lot better, and quick. After a couple of sessions of follow-the-leader, things opened up a bit and you were able to flex your wings. The track seemed like a familiar stretch of road, the squid traffic you were waiting behind all the time finally started to wick it up or plant their bikes in the weeds, and you were exploring speeds that would be suicidal on the street. This was also your first lesson, and the most valuable one, that you learned on the track: There is absolutely no place on the street for riding at 90 or 100 percent. After flogging your bike through the same dozen or so gravel- and puddle-free corners without worrying about oncoming cars, you realized how much risk you had been taking out there in the real world, and how much safer it was to do this in a track environment. Ka-ching! You've just doubled your life expectancy.

I learned some tricks right away. By the third session, my friends and I figured out that if we staged at the front of the line

and got out on the track first, we could go as fast as we wanted without waiting for Ricky Racer No. 929 every time he dropped anchor in the corners. When we caught up to the slowpokes, we just pulled into the pits, waited for the first one to come around again, then jumped out in front of them. Sweet.

By the end of the day, we were terrorizing the beginner group and earned our first testosterone-ego boost: a swift promotion to the intermediate group. The heads began to swell and I got my first sweet taste of what it's like to receive a reward for being faster than everyone else. Like that first taste of beer when I was in my teens or the first time some cute girl looked me up and down, that reward carried far more meaning to me than simply keeping from running up Joe Slow No. 916's tailpipes had. That reward meant I had something that someone else didn't. I liked it, and like a drug addict, had to have more. And soon. No matter what the price.

But I also learned that my bike was not suited so well for the track. I ran up against its limits right away and discovered it either needed some heavy modification or I needed a dedicated track bike. (Kiss the next eight paychecks goodbye!) I also discovered that my years of riding experience weren't enough either, but that, on the other hand, was a good thing. Just when I thought I knew everything there was to know about riding, I got to be a newbie once again (sort of like a "born-again virgin," only a hell of a lot faster). Just as I had to struggle and learn how to ride a street bike safely and efficiently at street speeds, then spend 13 years perfecting it, I discovered that I had to learn how to ride a race bike safely and efficiently on a racetrack—which means I get 13 more years of self-discovery! The joy of learning to ride a motorcycle—of perfecting your style and craft—can be had all over again with another big learning curve at the track. There's absolutely no price you can put on that.

So why am I running my pie hole about track days when this chapter is supposed to be about racing? Well, I want you to reminisce for a minute about your first track day. The smiles, the thrills, and of course, the need for speed. It hasn't gotten any better than that. Now think harder. Remember that late afternoon session when you finally had your turn-in points down and felt like you were on fire? Remember for that session that seemed to last for hours, that the track was yours and you owned every apex? You were some kind of motorcycle god, right? And then, out of nowhere on the second-to-last lap, some guy came by you on the outside of your favorite turn like you were sitting still. How did he *do* that? You must have done something wrong, because there's no *way* this guy is faster than you, right? So you put your head down and set your sights on passing him back. Everything else was blocked out of your mind. Your muscles had memorized the corners, the throttle, the bars, the brakes, and you just pushed a little harder and kept him in your scope. And then you passed him back, stuffing him into a decreasing-radius turn because you had the balls to outbrake him at 110 mph.

That, my friends, is the thrill of competition. You've now got the taste to race.

Any pass on the racetrack brings some satisfaction, but nothing is quite as satisfying as putting white-plate "experts" behind you while still running as a yellow-plated amateur. Tony Marx

A good race bike never dies—it just gets passed on to new owners while getting cheaper and cheaper with each exchange. Here is my former SV650 racer now with its fourth owner being thrashed by the fifth person to borrow it, Sheldon Nelson.
Tony Marx

The First Race Experience

For some of you, the excitement that track days offer will be plenty and you'll never want anything more. But some of you will want more—and the only place to get it is club-level racing. When I got bitten by the bug, I felt track days were ten times better than riding on the street. And just when I thought it couldn't get any better, Kent, my friendly neighborhood pusher, invited me to get my race license using his fully prepped GS500.

It took me about two seconds to accept his offer, and a couple of weeks later I was off to Mid-America Motorplex once again to get my license to run with the big boys in the Central Roadracing Association. I spent an entire Friday sitting in the classroom learning about the flags, start procedures, and track etiquette. The practice sessions that day were pretty straightforward and reminded me a lot of the track days I'd come to love. But I wanted more—after all I came here on the promise that this would be even more fun than track days.

Well, it took me the entire day to put it all together, but the "final exam" at the end of the day sealed the deal. We had about 15 new riders in my class that day on everything from GS500s to the latest and greatest 600-cc thoroughbreds, and even a couple of guys on liter-class twins. The final test for your race license is the new rider race. You don't have to place in the top five to be accepted, all you need to do is finish the race and you're home free. Screw that. I wasn't there to finish the race; I was there to win it. After all, if you're not worried about winning, then just do track days the rest of your life.

When you head out for a typical session at a track day, you're secretly learning to race. You line up at the entrance to the track, wait patiently in the heat with the motor growling, then the guy standing in your way of your favorite turns steps aside and you roll out onto the tarmac. The start of a race isn't much different—it's all in the way you look at it—except that it's better. Now you're not sitting in line next to a bunch of other guys out to have fun like you. No, now you're gridded next to other competitors. Your job is to make it around the track before they do. Racing isn't just an expensive outing with the guys anymore. These people you once considered friends have, for the time being, become the enemy, the lugheads and mouth-breathers you have to beat across that finish line—at any cost. My heart's pounding just writing about it.

But wait: This book isn't about me, it's about you. Here's how your new rider race plays out.

The flag drops and the group makes a mad dash for that first turn—absolute chaos. The guy next to you dumped his clutch a little too fast and stood his bike up in the twelve o'clock position, teetering back and forth like he might just come crashing down on top of somebody. The slower bikes like the GS you're riding are set at the back of the grid, and as you fear for your life, the rest of the grid uses their extra 50 horsepower to rush away from you like you're standing still. Hell, even the dumb ass that wheelied his bike managed to set it back down and pass you before turn 1. Now you're pissed—how *dare* these guys show up with faster bikes than yours?

Don't let it get you down, though. After all, racing is a challenge and you're going to make the most of it, and draw on every resource you have to smoke these guys. Since you're on a power-deprived but ultralight bike, the only hope you have is to be faster than these guys in the corners.

One by one you start to pick them off and work your way to the front. Unlike most track day organizations, there are no rules against passing in racing. If you can get that front tire into the corner first, then it's your line and to hell with anyone else that's in your way—and now you're really taking advantage of it. With your lighter bike, you late brake everyone you can into the corners, and then do your best to stay in their way so they can't get around you before the next corner comes up.

Like I did that day, you end up finishing the race in third place, and although you're a little bit disappointed that you didn't win it outright,

you are happy that you even finished the race at all—and on a smaller bike, to boot! It was terrifying, exhilarating, and nerve-wracking. Now it will take you a couple of minutes to come down from the high after that first race, and then it starts to really sink in. You completely lost yourself in those five laps of absolute bliss. You didn't think about anything but reeling them in and checking them off, one at a time. Your bills, broken-down truck, job, not even your love life crossed your mind during those five laps. You've now found something you can completely immerse yourself in, if only for a few laps at a time. You are now addicted to racing.

If doing a track day was ten times better than riding on the street for me, then it's pretty safe to say that racing was ten times better than doing a track day. Going as fast as I could was fun, but going faster than other people on comparable equipment was just awesome. Since I started racing, I've had some of the best highs and some of the worst lows in my life. It's no bed of roses, that's for sure. But when you cross that finish line in first place, or at least in front of the guy you've been battling with for eight laps, there's nothing better. On that day, in that race, you were the best guy on the track—or at

Supermotard has been making a comeback and can be a cheap and fun way to get into the racing scene. Jack Beaudry

Track day rules seldom allow passing mid-corner but that happens frequently during a race. Here Karl and Dave are in a heated battle through turn 10 at Brainerd International Raceway. Tony Marx

Two different laps have two different outcomes. Does it look better to be on the inside or the outside through this corner?
Tony Marx

least better than *that* guy—and nothing compares to that feeling of being number one.

Getting Started

So where will the sickness take you? Well, there are many different ways to go about getting into racing, so I'll give you a few pointers to make the most of your first year.

First and foremost: Gear up. Before you even think about spending some serious time and taking some serious chances on the track, your leathers, boots, gloves, and helmet have to be top-notch. If you have skimped on anything, it's time to go back and finish what you started. Get good gear—the best you can afford. The $80 you saved buying a pair of cheapo gloves that looked good won't mean much to you when half of your hand is ground off and the doctor tells you you're going to have to lose a finger. Eighty bucks is nothing compared to what that extra dough can do for you in a get off. There is advice in this book for buying and selecting gear. When in doubt, ask around at the track and find out what the fast guys are wearing.

Get your license. Your favorite track day provider can probably certify you, and if they can't, they can definitely recommend someone who can. Or you can let your browser do the walking and search the Internet for race schools. Beware, though: a race-certification class is a bit different from a track day. There's a lot about safety and rules that you need to know so you're not a complete menace to the other riders out there. Pay attention—this stuff can save your life, or somebody else's.

Your best bet is to plan on spending the entire day in a classroom with your hand in the air, asking questions, learning about protective gear and flags and some basic track riding tips. (If you've done a few track days and read a few books, you'll know more than three-quarters of the people in the class.) Imagine yourself in school again, waiting for the clock to strike three so you could hit the playground. Once you're accustomed to that idea, plan on getting a little time at the end of the day to ride on the track to get certified—the new rider race.

If you can be happy with that, you'll be thrilled with most race certification schools, which will probably give you at least three or four sessions to get your ya-yas out, and finish you off with a race license to boot.

Find a racing club. There are lots of them to choose from. Let your browser do the walking.

The Machine

For your rookie season, start small. Although it was very tempting for me to cut my race teeth on an RC51, the best thing I ever did was accept the offer to use my friend's GS500. The bike was slow, didn't handle very well, and to make matters even worse, the thing was bad ugly. But that GS taught me more than my cocky brain thought possible.

Starting out on a small bike has a lot of advantages. At the club level, there's always an ultralight or lightweight class designed specifically for smaller bikes like the GS500 and SV650 and that's due mainly to one thing: the low cost of smaller bikes puts them more easily within the reach of new racers. These bikes are significantly cheaper than the current crop of 600s, and if you dig around a little bit, you can find a decent specimen for less than $3,000. And that's not all. Because they only make 50 to 70 horsepower, they're a lot easier on tires, so that spendy race rubber will last you a whole lot longer. You can buy a pair of tires for the season instead of hoping a set will last the weekend. And, of course, if you should crash the bike and completely demolish it, you're only out a couple grand. Just go buy another one. Or better yet, buy a spare so you can keep racing the same day you wad up your first one.

Beyond the cost advantages, though, there's a lot to learn on a small bike. Although gobs of horsepower can be a lot of fun, it also has a tendency to cover up a lot of mistakes you might make when you first start racing. Don't trade power for skill, especially when you're starting out. Riding a small bike makes you really pay attention to the finer details of going fast. When you don't have a hundred or so horsepower to make up for your errors, you have no choice but to do things right the first time. You have to late brake your opponents, or carry more corner speed, if you really want to get to the front of the pack. Anything you learn about cornering, braking, passing, drafting, or planning on an underpowered bike can be transferred directly over to a more powerful bike when you're ready to move up in classes.

My first race bike was an SV650. I had started on my buddy's GS500, and although I'd had a blast on it getting my license and showing the other newbies what-for, I needed just a little more

There is usually someone around who will step up and help you get your bike on or off the rear stand. However, with some practice, this is a one person job. If your track bike no longer has its kickstand, put in the practice so you can get your bike on the stand without looking like a spaz or dropping your bike. Susan Larson

Getting a knee down will happen. Don't make it an obsession. Just work on good cornering technique and proper body positioning, and before you know it the ground will be right there in your knee's way. Mark Miller

speed and power to keep me interested. The SV was a street bike that landed in my lap at an amazing price with some road rash from a pretty mild crash. If you look around, you'll find dozens of worthy specimens just ripe for the conversion. You can then settle down to spend the winter tearing down the bike to the frame and motor and getting rid of everything that doesn't help make it go fast, and turn it into a real race bike.

Making the Most of Your Machine

You can always just safety wire a stock bike and race it, but if you want to be competitive (and become intimately familiar with your ride), you're going to need to make some modifications. Walk around the track on a race weekend and you'll see everything from wild to mild. There'll be guys who have spent the bare minimum on their bikes, to guys who have put a second mortgage on their house to buy every trick part known to man. What you do to your bike is up to you, but there are going to be a few obvious things that need to be done. I was on a budget, so what I did had as much to do with my financial limitations as it did my desire to humiliate people on the track. If you're on a budget or don't want to invest too much before you decide for sure that racing is for you, pay attention.

The first thing I did was make sure the suspension on the bike was the best I could afford. Next to riding skill, cornering is all

about suspension—not power. I purchased a very nice shock and had my front forks completely overhauled by Traxxion Dynamics. What you spend your money on is obviously up to you, but if you're going to dump any money into your bike, spend it on suspension first. I know I keep harping on this point, but horsepower is not really where it's at when you're first starting out. Having a good-handling machine underneath you is what's really going to help you learn how to ride.

If you have your suspension set up by a professional shop such as Traxxion Dynamics, your bike should come back to you in a condition that is pretty close to what you need. If you decide to do it yourself, make sure you do your research first. You can spend $2,000 on a great shock, but if it's not set up for your weight and application, it'll be completely useless. Ride height is something else that can make a huge difference in the way the bike handles. It's a good idea to start out with the bike as close to stock as possible both front and rear to see what it feels like and then make adjustments from there.

While the suspension was in Max's capable hands, I slapped in a new set of sintered metal brake pads up front to handle the extreme braking of racing. I took my rims to the local race rubber distributor and had a set of the stickiest tires I could afford installed. Race rubber is quite a bit different than the stuff you're used to running on the street. Not only is the traction ten times better, but the profiles are usually a lot more extreme and help your bike turn-in a lot faster. The tires from each manufacturer have their own characteristics so ask a lot of questions when you buy your first set and don't be afraid to try a couple of different brands to find the one that suits your riding style the best.

Next, I completely gutted the bike. Depending on the model of bike, there's actually an opportunity to get some of your money back here. The SV I purchased was the S model with the fairing, so all the stock bodywork went up on eBay and netted me $500 to put back into the bike. Then I proceeded to pull everything off the bike that wasn't absolutely necessary. Check the rules of the club you plan to race with, but if they don't say you need it, then toss it. Although that little 3-ounce bracket you just threw in the box doesn't make a huge impact by itself, keep adding up the parts you've pulled off and you can easily shave 10 to 15 pounds off the bike. Remember, in racing light is right, and 10 or 15 pounds can mean 1 or 2 horsepower, depending on where it comes from.

Once I had the bike stripped down, it was time to rebuild it as a full-on race machine. I was lucky—my bike came with a full race exhaust system already installed—so I didn't have to worry about buying an exhaust for it. But if you're converting a stock bike into a racer, think hard about streamlining your exhaust system—header, pipe, everything. Let that baby breathe and shave off another 10 to 15 pounds in the process. Plus it looks really cool.

As soon as I got my suspension back and had the bike rolling, I took it to my local race tuner. I didn't want to spend a whole lot of money on the bike, and luckily I didn't have to. I had my tuner install a timing advancer and set the carburetors up so that the bike ran perfectly. When he was done I had about five more horses and a perfect air-to-fuel ratio all the way through the rev range—all for just a little more than $300.

The fun in building a race bike is all the cool stuff available for it. To make the SV look like the race bike it was going to be, I got a set of race bodywork. Besides a few vintage-only clubs, most require a full belly pan capable of retaining at least 5 quarts of fluid—backup in case your motor should decide to puke oil or water all over the race line. If you're prepping a 600 sportbike, this is no big deal, but for smaller bikes that didn't come with full bodywork, this is something you need to address. My full race bodywork had a belly pan so my problem was solved. For those of you who don't want to go that route, you can get creative, and cheap—I've even seen aluminum foil turkey-basting pans safety wired under the bike pass tech inspection. Check with the club you're going to race with before you try something like that, though. Failing tech inspection your first weekend because you didn't read the rules is not fun.

So I had the big stuff covered and the bike was starting to come together nicely, but there were still a million things to wrap up. I put a new chain and sprockets on the bike, and converted it to a 520 chain while I was at it to save a little weight. The new suspension raised the rear ride height, lowered the front, and created a bike that turned in a lot better—but was also a little twitchy mid-corner. I splurged and added a steering damper to keep it nice and smooth. I managed to get a couple hundred bucks for the stock gauges, so I added a digital tachometer and electronic shift light to help keep the bike in the rev range. I was beginning to spend money like a drunken sailor, but it was fun to have the slick technology at my disposal. And to monitor my progress, I also added a lap timer to the cockpit so I knew exactly how fast I was going out on the track. When you're learning, a lap timer is a huge help. If you can't afford one, borrow one, or bribe your little brother to stand there with a stopwatch during practice.

There were a few other add-ons that aren't going to win you any beauty pageants, but are still pretty necessary. I swapped out the stock footpegs with aftermarket rear sets made by Woodcraft. The big advantage to rear sets is that they move the pegs up and back, giving you added cornering clearance and putting your lower body in a better position to move around on the bike—your legs become like coiled springs. Up front, I pulled the stock handlebars off and added a set of billet clip-ons with replaceable bars. These usually move the bars down and forward, again, helping to make the seating position a little more aggressive. Sitting on the bike, legs coiled, arms ready to take a swing, you'll look like a jungle cat ready to strike. The other big benefit is that the bars are replaceable, so when you crash you can simply pull the bent one off and replace it and have the bike ready to go in a matter of minutes. That came in very, very handy for me during my first year. And my second.

Don't Forget the Little Things

With all the cool parts I could afford installed, it was time to get down to the small details. Racing puts a lot of stress on a motorcycle. You'll be running it up to red line multiple times in a lap, and then compounding things by running lap after lap. The bike will vibrate and things will start to come loose. That's where safety wire comes in.

All clubs require you to use safety wire to one extent or another. My advice is to use the stuff everywhere possible to make sure you don't lose important parts of your bike at the wrong time. For the CRA, I was required to safety wire the oil drain plug and filler cap, the oil filter, the brake caliper mounting bolts, and the axle pinch bolts on the front. In addition to that, I safety wired the exhaust hanger bolt, the banjo bolts on the brake lines, and the pin on the rear axle castle nut. A generous helping of Loctite on everything else to make sure the bike holds together and she's all set.

After the bike is all assembled and good to go, it's time to add the cool touches. I pulled the bodywork off and sent it to a paint shop. The tank was still perfect so I had them color match the

On the street this could get you a ticket for exhibition, careless driving, or reckless driving, with fines ranging from $50 to $200 and a possible impound of your ride. At the track this will get you smiles and other affirmations or at most a "we don't allow that here" warning. Tony Marx

factory blue and do the rest of the bodywork in the same color. If you're lucky enough to find a sponsor willing to give you some money to feed your hobby, they might have a say in what your bike ends up looking like. If not, have fun with it. Your paint is the only thing that separates you from the rest of the pack. I've seen everything from military-style camouflage to a pink bike with black spots to simulate a pig.

Building a bike is pretty much a fun process, but make sure you give yourself plenty of time. You have read through this far, and it seems like it's a breeze—and honestly, it should be. But it doesn't always happen that way, so plan ahead and allow time for complications. Plus, if you're ever hurting for spring to roll around, if winter seems like it's just going to last forever, just sign up for an expensive, non-refundable track day in early spring, sell your old track bike, and build a new track bike. If you've ever wanted to speed up time, this is the trick: It's amazing how all the little things add up, and before you know it, you've got two days to put the thing together before the first race weekend! I was lucky and had all winter to build my first one. By the time the first weekend rolled around, all I had to do was purge out the antifreeze from winter storage and refill it with straight water. You should be so lucky.

Your best bet when starting this process is to get a copy of the rules from the club you're going to be racing with. Read through the bike requirements section and start making a list of everything you'll need to do to your bike. Then add to the list all the aftermarket stuff you can't live without, including the prices, and factor in some money for tuning the bike as well. When you're done, you'll have a nice checklist to make sure your bike has everything it needs, and an idea of the kind of money you'll need to finish it. Like I said, give yourself plenty of time to get it all wrapped up and leave a little extra for the unexpected.

Checklist (In Order of Priority)
Riding gear
Race certification school
Small track bike
New rear shock
Rebuild front forks
Upgrade front brake pads
Install race tires
Strip bike of unnecessary parts
Replace exhaust
Tune bike
Race bodywork or belly pan
Chain and sprockets
Steering damper
Shift light
Lap timer
Rear sets
Clip-ons
Safety wire
Coolant
Paint

The Payoffs

There is one other big difference between track days and racing, and that's contingency money; that is, money manufacturers pay to racers who win using their products. It's definitely something to consider as you get ready to build your bike. After all, it can put money in your pocket for the parts you need to keep racing. Every club has a different list of companies that offer contingency, so check with them to see what's offered. When I built my first bike, I went out of my way to run products that paid contingency in my club. You might not get much, but a few bucks in your pocket for things like tires and brake pads can go a long way.

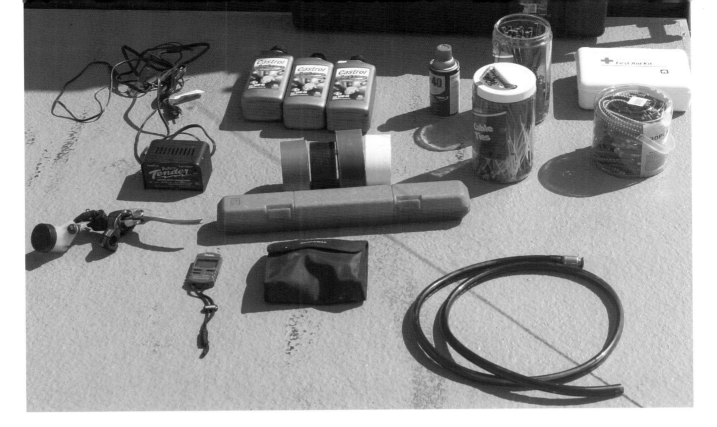

A bunch of zip ties, duct tape, WD40, and other miscellaneous items like a battery charger, spare levers, and a torque wrench are always good to have on hand. Kent Larson

For a lot of riders, racing isn't just a hobby or an addiction; it becomes a lifestyle. I've made some of my best friends at the track; people I consider brothers and sisters. Your friends, family, and co-workers will probably think you're crazy for doing this—and honestly they're at least somewhat right. You've got to be a little off to want to put a knee on the pavement at triple digits! Realizing that everyone around you at the track is a little off, too, is what makes it such a high.

On the other side, racing can have some pretty big lows as well. I put a lot of time and effort into building that first bike only to crash it my second race weekend of the year. It hurts to spend that much time and pour in that much of your effort and then see your baby tumbling down the track. To make matters worse, the bike came down on my left hand and mangled it pretty bad. Now I've got a middle finger that looks like a coat hanger and I lost the top third of my ring finger. Most people will tell you if something like that happened to them they'd be long gone from the sport. But racers are a different breed—we're a little off, remember. For me, it was just one more challenge in the game that I had to overcome to beat those other guys.

But those were only temporary setbacks. I managed to get the bike put back together, and seven weeks later I was stuffing my still-mangled and swollen hand into a new glove so I could get back out on the track. It hurt like hell, and caused me a lot of problems, but I still had a smile on my face when I got off the track. You can walk around the pits at a racetrack on any weekend and hear a hundred stories just like that. Guys with broken bones, stitches, and duct-taped leathers are out there beating up themselves and their bikes chasing that checkered flag. And smiling the whole time.

So what should you take away from all this? Well, just be aware that what you're about to do might possibly change your life forever—for good or bad. What you're about to do is not going to be easy, but nothing as rewarding as this is easy. You'll make some great friends, you might even band together and start a race team with a funny name such as Team Poop dot org. You'll probably never be famous, you'll probably end up crashing a time or two (or four), and you might even get hurt. Badly. But when you cross that finish line for your first time in the lead, with 15 or 20 of the fastest guys you know behind you, it takes you three hours to wipe the grin off your face and it all becomes worth it.

It's time to put up or shut up, contact your local road racing club and see what you've got.

MotoGP, here I come!

TRACK DAY ORGANIZATIONS AND TRACK SCHOOLS

There are hundreds of track day organizations throughout the world, most in the United States and western Europe. Choosing a track and an organization or school should be based on what you hope to learn, your level of experience, your confidence level, the condition and quality of your bike and riding gear, and your comfort level at higher speeds. Some whiners might complain that there are too many choices. The rest of us think it's a nice problem to have. In reality, finding the right track event for you should be as easy as spending an hour searching the Internet. Read carefully.

A quick Web search will turn up more track day events than you can possibly attend in a lifetime. A Google search for "motorcycle track day" will get you a surprisingly long listing. "European motorcycle track day" (or "U.S. motorcycle track day," if you're in Europe) will nearly double that list, if you're in the mood for a serious travel vacation. If you're looking for something in your region, include that in your search as well (Georgia, Midwest, United Kingdom, etc.). If you're more interested in track schools than open track days, substitute "school" for "day" and let your browser do the walking. By the time you've decided which school you're going to first, you'll probably already have numbers two through eight picked out, and you'll be looking carefully at your checkbook with high hopes.

General Bike Requirements

At a minimum, all track organizations require you to have a safe machine that doesn't spew various fluids across the landscape, and most require you to pass a tech inspection. Basic open and controlled track days require a minimum of preparation because they cater to riders on street machines. A full race prep requirement would be safer and benefit everyone with shorter post-bike-toss down times. However, the basic track day provider knows that requiring a race prep would drain the potential customer pool. If the business is going to float, that pool needs to be as large as possible. The new client is usually not asked for any more prep than removing mirrors and taping all the glass (headlights) and hard plastic (taillights, signals, reflectors) so that a bike toss doesn't leave a lot of shattered bits to pick up before riding can resume.

ome organizations don't even require the shatter protection tape. The Northeast Sportbike Association (www.nesba.com), for example, requires nothing more from their intro group than a safety check. You can ride your well-maintained street bike right onto the track once the safety check provides you with a sticker on the headlight to show you passed.

Track schools and race schools sometimes require additional preparation, but rarely approach that of full-on race prep. Schools that are serious about bike setup typically have bikes that are ready to be flogged available for the purpose—at a price. Many will find it well worth the price.

For an insignificant $200 premium (plus damage deposit), you can have a day on a professionally prepped Kawasaki 600 with the California Superbike School (www.superbikeschool.com). Going with other organizations can buy you a ride on most of the current 600-cc rockets. Ride Honda with Freddie Spencer's High Performance Riding School (www.fastfreddie.com), or Suzuki with Kevin Schwantz Suzuki School (www.schwantzschool.com). Cost of class and bike rental can run from $600 to over $2,000, but the chance to see what your bike would feel like when set up properly or the opportunity to sample a "perfect" example before buying can be worth it. Besides, the bike sampling is just a bonus on top of world-class training from motorsport legends.

When attending a track day or school in which you are riding your own bike, be sure to show up with a full tank of gas and a few extra gallons on the side. If you are riding with an efficient organization and cutting fast laps, it would not be unusual to add 300 miles to your odometer by the end of the day. Track miles gobble gas faster than street miles. Your 44 miles-per-gallon machine will now be making about 37 or 38 mpg so plan accordingly. A bike will typically drop about 15 percent off its casual street riding efficiency when being flogged aggressively about a racetrack.

Specific Bike Requirements

There are two basic sets of bike requirements: track street prep and track race prep. Club racing bike preparation is usually quite a bit more involved than both of these.

Street Prep Bike Requirements

Tires should be newer with at least 75 percent tread life left. Worn, damaged, or dry-rotted tires are not acceptable, regardless of tread life.

Brakes should be in top condition, front and rear. They should give good pressure feedback and have adequate pad thickness with no fluid leaks.

Chain and sprockets should not be worn out to the extreme, and chain should be properly tensioned and lubed with no rust or damage.

Headlights, taillights, and mirrors are generally required to be taped over or removed. Many organizations require removal or taping over of turn signals, speedometer, and wheel weights.

Clip-on bars, footpegs, exhaust, and bodywork must be securely fastened to the bike. Controls such as the throttle must be self-closing. Most organizations require an operational kill switch at the thumb.

Race Prep Bike Requirements

All the street prep requirements, plus:
Oil drain plug, fill cap, and filter must be safety wired.
Antifreeze replaced with water or approved coolant.

General Rider/Protective Gear Requirements

Few organizations have requirements for the rider's experience level or licensure, but every organization will be strict regarding the rider's protective gear. At a bare minimum, plan on leaving none of your skin exposed. Required gear includes the following:

- Full-faced helmet with a DOT, Snell, or Gold Stamp
- One- or two-piece leather zip-together riding suit. Heavy-duty, motorcycle-specific textile riding suits are generally acceptable (Aerostich Roadcrafter, First Gear, etc.).
- Leather gloves that cover the wrist
- Sturdy leather motorcycle boots. Some of the open and controlled organizations allow high-top sneakers.

Track Organizations

The rest of this chapter is devoted to examples and information for several different track organizations, including open, controlled, and school/race organizations. For each entry, you'll find the type of organization, contact information, a general description of what to expect, and general (and specific) requirements. Since there are far more organizations than can be adequately covered here (and many more are there and gone in the blink of an eye!), these are some of the more respected, long-lived, and representative samples of what you'll find when you search the Web.

My website, www.larsonroadracing.com, attempts to keep a list of track day organizations available in the United States along with descriptions and reviews. With your help, this resource will be maintained as a comprehensive updated list of who provides track time. Contact kent_larson@comcast.net with reviews and notes on errors or omissions.

Open Track Days

SoCal Track Days, LLC (www.socaltrackdays.com, 760-360-2834) is a newer track organization providing open track days for experienced riders and training for CCS racing licenses. SoCal operates exclusively at Spring Mountain Motorsports Park in Pahrump, Nevada, 40 miles west of Las Vegas.

Bike requirements: Standard street prep.

Special bike preparation: Minimum 250-cc displacement, safety wire recommended but not required.

Rider requirements: Standard protective gear.

Special rider requirements: All riders must have previous racetrack experience from a recognized school or racing organization. Also, Joe Rocket "Phoenix" or similar lightweight suits are not acceptable.

Simplicity, freedom, and maximum track time are the guiding principles of SoCal Track Days. Started in January 2003 with the mission of providing an open track day environment for experienced motorcycle riders, SoCal uses a no-session format that allows riders the opportunity for maximum track time with minimum hassles. The goal is to provide a safe, smooth, and satisfying track experience and the freedom for riders to set their own agenda and sufficient track time to accomplish their goals.

Keigwins@theTrack (www.keigwin.com, 650-949-5609) offers open track time, as well as novice, advanced, and racing schools at Infineon, Thunderhill, Laguna Seca, Reno-Fernley, and Buttonwillow. The different formats for Keigwins track days offer something for every rider's sensibility, and they're very strict on safety.

Bike requirements: Standard street prep.

Special bike requirements: Antifreeze must be replaced with water or approved coolant, and 6-inch numbers are required at Laguna Seca.

Rider requirements: Standard protective gear.

Special rider requirements: Track experience is required for all groups except novice.

One of the larger track organizations in the western United States, Keigwins offers inexpensive access to high-resolution digital photographers, DVD videography, professional suspension setup, and lap timer rentals. Keigwins also offers free tire changing and balancing the week before the track event and delivery of any parts and/or supplies directly to the racetrack from their full-service motorcycle shop.

TrackAddix (www.trackaddix.com, 888-234-4740) offers no-session track days at Brainerd International Raceway, Heartland Park, Mid-America Motorplex, Pike's Peak International Raceway, and Spring Mountain Motorsports Park. "No sessions" means the track is open from 9 a.m. until 6 p.m. with an hour break for lunch and for riders to walk the track for a closer view. Otherwise, riders can get on and off the track at will. TrackAddix also offers video recording services and lap timers, among other services.

Bike requirements: Standard street prep on the honor system (no tech inspection); wiring the drain bolts and caps is highly recommended.

Rider requirements: Standard protective gear.

Special rider requirements: Previous track experience required.

SpeedFreak Track Days (www.speedfreaktrackdays.com, 01625-859969) offers track time at Brands Hatch Indy, Coldwell Full Circuit, Croft, Donington GP, Donington National, Lydd Raceway, Mallory, Oulton Park, Silverstone

GP, Silverstone National, Snetterton, and Three Sisters.

Bike requirements: Standard street prep.

Rider requirements: Standard protective gear.

Hyperclub Track Days (www.hypercycle.com, 818-988-8860) offers track days at Willow Springs 2.5 Mile, and the Streets of Willow Springs. Interference and preparation are minimal and experts (AMA riders) are available for free advice on riding skills, technique, tires, suspension, etc.

Bike requirements: Standard street prep but a thorough tech inspection.

Rider requirements: Standard protective gear.

Other Open Track Day Organizations

Apex Trackdays (USA), www.apextrackdays.com

CanyonStrafers (USA), www.canyonstrafers.com

Hammy Boys Motosports (USA), www.hammyboys.com

Knockhill Racing Circuit (UK), www.knockhill.co.uk

Monster Jockey (France), www.monsterjockey.com

The Motorcycle Folly (UK), www.motorcyclefolly.co.uk

MTC Track Day (USA), www.mtctrackday.com

No Limits Track Days (UK, Europe),
        www.nolimitstrackdays.com

Phil Bevan Racing (UK), www.philbevanracing.co.uk

Track Daz (USA), www.trackdaz.com

Track Sense (UK), www.tracksense.co.uk

Track Tamers (UK), www.tracktamers.co.uk

Controlled Track Days

Northeast Sportbike Association (www.nesba.com, 877-AT-NESBA) is one of the most prolific track day organizations in the world. With almost 100 track days each year, NESBA is the largest sportbike track day organization in the United States, providing instruction and safe, controlled track time for motorcycle riders. NESBA offers the most opportunities and venues to ride in the Northeast, Mid-Atlantic, Southeast, Midwest, and Northwest United States. Whether you're a street rider or a racer, NESBA has something for you.

Bike requirements: Standard street prep.

Special bike requirements: Intro group must tape over or disconnect the rear brake lights. Beginner and Intermediate groups must remove mirrors and tape over all lights and reflectors. Advanced group must safety wire the oil drain plug, oil fill cap, and oil filter as well as replace the coolant with water (Evans Cooling or Engine Ice is not allowed). All groups are encouraged to prep to the Advanced group requirements.

Rider requirements: Standard protective gear.

Special rider requirements: Intro group is allowed to ride using two pairs of jeans instead of leather or heavy textile pants. Back protector is strongly recommended.

Pending weather and safety conditions, members can expect about seven to nine 20-minute track sessions per event. To ensure safety and to maintain a controlled environment, all riders are grouped into riding levels according to their skill level and the number of participants per level is limited. Some minor bike preparation is required, depending on riding level. These levels make your ride time more enjoyable.

NESBA uses control riders to ensure rider safety and event control. They are the pace keepers of the track. Control riders are also present for riders to use as instructors, so ask them questions and get feedback. They can tell you what you're doing wrong and how you can improve your current skills.

Skill levels at NESBA events

Intro: This free trial level was created for the street rider not sure about signing up for a full day of riding. The intro level rider receives the beginner classroom session and has access to the track for two 15- to 20-minute Beginner sessions in the morning rotation. There is no bike preparation requirement; however, participants will be required to pass tech inspection.

Beginner: This level is very structured and geared toward those who have little or no experience riding on a track. A classroom session gets participants acquainted with the track. Control riders act as instructors and set the pace. Passing is limited. With each session, the group is guaranteed a steady increase in speed throughout the day.

Intermediate: This level is less supervised and structured. Control riders look at riding ability and encourage faster or slower riders to move up or down a level. Passing is allowed everywhere except in corners. The structure of this group may change to more closely resemble either the advanced or beginner group, depending on the group's riding ability.

Advanced: This level has very little supervision. Control riders are present to spot unsafe riding maneuvers. Passing is allowed anywhere on the track. This level is run much like an open racing practice.

LockhartPhillipsUSA.com Sport Rider Track Days (www.FormulaUSA.com, 817-332-4822) is the current incarnation of the Championship Cup Series (CCS) track events that have been available for 21 years. CCS and LP Privateer Sport Rider Days include affiliate agreements with Team Hammer, STAR School, California Superbike School, Learning Curves, Mid-America Riders, Keigwins at the Track, SoCal Track Days, Church of Speed, and FastTrax, and offer controlled track days, racing schools, and licensing clinics.

Bike requirements:

Street classes: Standard street prep.

Race classes: Standard race prep.

Rider requirements: Standard protective gear for street or race groups.

CCS and affiliates offer track time at all major road race courses in North America, including Barber Motorsports Park, Blackhawk Farms, Brainerd International Raceway, Buttonwillow, California Speedway, Carolina Motorsports Park, Cresson Motorsports Ranch, Daytona International Speedway, Firebird International Raceway, Gateway International Raceway, Gingerman Raceway, Grattan Raceway, Hallet Raceway, Heartland Park, Homestead-Miami Raceway, Laguna Seca Raceway, Las Vegas Motor Speedway, Mid-America Motorplex, Moroso Motorsports Park, Nelson Ledges, New Hampshire International Speedway, Jennings GP, No Problem Raceway, Oak Hill Raceway, Phoenix International Raceway, Pocono International Raceway, Portland International Raceway, Putnum Park Raceway, Road America, Road Atlanta, Roebling Road Raceway, Streets of Willow, Summit Point Raceway, Texas World Speedway, Thunderhill Park, Virginia International Raceway, and Willow Springs International Raceway.

For more than 21 years, CCS has provided top-level sportsman racing from coast to coast. Racing classes include rules for every motorcycle ever built, and more than $12 million in race contingency awards are available.

CCS events are included in 10 different regions from coast to coast at the same courses used in the Lockhart-PhillipsUSA.com Sport Rider Track Days.

100% Bikes (www.100pc.co.uk, 0870-8722532) offers safe and controlled track days at courses all over the United Kingdom and Europe: Croft, Oulton Park, Donington, Caldwell Park, Pembrey, Mallory Park, Rockingham, Snetterton, Silverstone, Brands Hatch, Lydd, Anglesey, Albacete, Almeria, Cartagena, Jerez, Monza, and Nogaro. The emphasis is on safety and skill development, and instructors are available at no cost. Photography and video services are also available.

Bike requirements: Minimal standard street prep.

Rider requirements: Standard protective gear.

Special rider requirements: Riders must have a motorcycle license, titanium knee and toe sliders are not permitted.

Tony's Track Days (www.TonysTrackDays.com) uses New Hampshire International Speedway to give the average street rider—not road racers or track junkies—a safe, non-competitive opportunity to enhance their skills in an environment free of the dangers and distractions of public roads. Racing, riding aggressively, and timing of laps are not allowed, and rules for passing are strict.

Bike requirements: Standard street prep.

Rider requirements: Standard protective gear.

Special rider requirements: Body armor in riding suit. High-top sneakers not allowed.

Lone Star Track Days (www.lonestartrackdays.com, 713-253-2966) has been providing track time for more than three years at Texas World Speedway and The Motorsport Ranch. Lone Star offers a riding school, as well as the CMRA Racing License School. Riders are divided into three groups by skill level. There are rules for passing, the emphasis is on track riding and skill development, and racing behavior is discouraged.

Bike requirements: Standard street.

Special bike requirements: 50 percent tire tread, no bikes smaller than 125-cc two-stroke, oil filter wire-tie recommended.

Rider requirements: Standard protective gear.

New York Sportbike Club, Inc. (www.nysportbikeclub.com, 516-921-5934), an East Coast track event organizer operating at Pocono Raceway, Summit Point Raceway, and Valley Motorsports Park, has been providing track time for three years and running.

Bike requirements: Standard street.

Special bike requirements: Tires must also have at least 28 psi of tire pressure, antifreeze must be replaced with water for the advanced group.

Rider requirements: Standard protective gear.

Special rider requirements: Back protector is required in advanced classes.

Other Controlled Track Day Organizations

Adrenaline Freaks (USA), www.adrenalinefreaks.com

Castle Combe Racing School (UK),
www.castlecomberacingschool.co.uk

Club Desmo (USA), www.clubdesmo.com

Club Zoom Zoom (USA), www.zoomzoomtrackdays.com

Darley Moor (UK), www.darleymoor.co.uk

Focused Events (UK, Europe), www.focusedevents.com

Gold Track (UK), www.goldtrack.co.uk

Hawaii Road Race Association (USA), www.hrra.net

Hottrax (UK), www.hottrax.co.uk

Kirkistown Track Days (UK),
www.kirkistowntrackdays.co.uk

Lydd International Raceway (UK),
www.lyddinternationalraceway.com

NASA Sport Bikes (USA), www.nasanornev.com

Northeast Sport Bike Association (USA),
www.nesba.com

Pacific Super Sport Riders (USA), www.PSSRtrack.com

Pacific Track Time (USA), www.pacifictracktime.com

Reduc Sportbike Association (USA), www.reduc.com

Sandia Motorcycle Roadracing, Inc. (USA),
www.smri-racing.org

Span Trax (Spain), www.spantrax.co.uk

T.E.A.M Arizona Tracktime (USA), www.aztracktime.com

Track Attack (UK), www.donington-park.co.uk

Track Time Promotions (UK),
www.tracktimepromotions.co.uk

Track Schools

The California Superbike School (www.superbikeschool.com, 323-224-2734) is probably the most widely known track school in the world. Operating in 11 countries and all across the United States, the California Superbike School has pioneered, refined, and provided its step-by-step rider training system to more than 100,000 riders and run over 4 million track miles since its beginning in 1980.

Bike requirements: Decent tires and a tank full of gas.

Rider requirements: Standard protective gear.

Keith Code, the school's director, has personally trained dozens of national, international, and regional racing champions; invented numerous rider training devices; and written three best-selling books on advanced rider training, *A Twist of the Wrist*, *A Twist of the Wrist II*, and *The Soft Science of Roadracing Motorcycles*. Before his works, there wasn't any unified training material available for the cornering enthusiast anywhere in the world.

Expect a well-organized, highly qualified, knowledgeable, and professional training and support staff. Each student is assigned to an instructor who provides coaching throughout the day for all on-track activities. Code himself has rarely missed a school in 25 years and generally does the technical briefings. The instructor/student ratio is between 2 and 4 to 1, depending on school format chosen.

The Superbike School's one- and two-day courses offer a highly methodical and structured approach to cornering. By breaking the actions of riding down into their simplest parts and approaching them one at a time, riders achieve new levels of confidence based on defined skills. The school's tag phrase, "Cornering—Learn the skills, Discover the Art," is based on real-world experience. The school has four levels of training, each comprised of five or more very specific drills. The on-track sessions are uncrowded because group size is limited; only 13 to 20 riders maximum are allowed per session, depending on the format chosen.

Based on availability, riders may ride their own bikes or choose one of the school's fleet of track prepped, Dunlop shod, current model, ZX-6R Kawasakis for their training. All riding gear is available for rental. Lap timers are also an option at a nominal charge. Snacks, electrolytes, beverages, printed course curriculum, and ear plugs are provided.

United Sport Bike Association (www.rideUSBA.com, 765-349-1070) has provided track days and rider clinics for nearly seven years. The USBA focus and goal is to increase the rider's knowledge and ability and provide a base of useful information for all riders, especially novice riders. USBA uses Putnam Park Road Course in Mount Meridian, Indiana.

Bike requirements: Minimal standard street prep.

Special bike requirements: Bikes must be 250 cc or greater, and antifreeze must be replaced with water or approved coolant.

Rider requirements: Standard protective gear.

Special rider requirements: Back protector.

USBA focuses on novice riders and provides instruction that combines classroom and track time. Safety is the primary concern, so the USBA doesn't tolerate abusive riding, violation of track rules, or improper conduct by any rider. The rider clinics focus on various critical riding skills to produce a more confident, controlled, and safer rider on the track and the street. A brief informal orientation begins the day, getting riders familiar with the facility and safety regulations. Instructors are assigned to each group (novice, intermediate, and advanced) to provide hands-on instruction and riding tips at the end of each riding session.

Jennings GP (www.jenningsgp.com, 386-938-1110)

uses a 2-mile, 14-turn, motorcycle-only, grand-prix-style track in northern Florida.

Bike requirements: Minimal standard street prep.

Special bike requirements: Bike noise can be no more than 104 decibels.

Rider requirements: Standard protective gear.

Operating two weekends a month year-round, Jennnings GP caters to those looking for no-hassle track time at a dedicated course, those looking for professional instruction, and those looking to get a license to race. They even provide low-key "mock races" for riders interested in trying their hand at racing. The primary goal of this organization is to provide a safe environment to broaden the sport of track riding and help keep high speeds and racing off the street.

A track orientation class is available free of charge for novices; leathers, boots, and gloves are available for rent; there are tire sales and mounting services; photography and concessions plus camping and showers are available. Track entry is free.

European Superbike School (www.europeansuperbikeschool.com, 0870-241-5159) offers open and controlled track days, and various levels of serious training at Cartagena, Croix En Ternois, Jerez, Brands Hatch, Nogaro, and Snetterton. Schools use video cameras, and run from basic, one-day courses to advanced two-day courses with world-renowned instructors and small student-to-instructor ratios. They also offer help with suspension setup, maintenance, preparation, tires, repairs, and tuning.

Bike requirements: Current MOT certificate and all glass must be taped.

Rider requirements: Standard protective gear.

Special rider requirements: Helmet must be less than three years old if not Gold Stamped.

Ride Smart (www.ridesmart.info, 512-469-9491) offers open practice and multiple levels of riding instruction in the Ty Howard Racing School. For four years they have operated at Texas World Speedway, the Motorsport Ranch, Texas Motor Speedway, and Hallett.

Bike requirements: Standard street prep.

Rider requirements: Standard protective gear.

Ride Smart's philosophy is for street riders to learn more control and learn from experts as well as themselves, using photography and video to give riders an opportunity to analyze their positioning and lines. Their race school is not a licensing clinic, but an advanced instruction in high-performance track techniques. Leathers, boots, and lap timers are available for rental. Ride Smart can also track lap times in a database for riders to see their improvement over time.

Other Track Schools

CLASS (USA), www.classrides.com

Cornerspeed Riderschool (USA), www.cornerspeed.net

dP Safety School (USA), www.dpsafetyschool.com

Ducati Riding Experience (Italy), www.ducati.com

Edge Performance Riding Courses (USA), www.edgeracing.net

FastTrax (USA), www.fastone.com

Freddie Spencer's High Performance Riding School (USA), www.fastfreddie.com

Grand Prix Riding Academy (Australia), www.grandprixacademy.com

Jason Pridmore's STAR (USA), www.starmotorcycle.com

Kevin Schwantz Suzuki School (USA), www.schwantzschool.com

Learning Curves (USA), www.learningcurves.com

Penguin Roadracing School (USA), www.penguinracing.com

Team Hammer (USA), www.teamhammer.com

Team Pro-Motion (USA), www.teampromotion.com

2Fast (USA), www.2-fast.org

INDEX

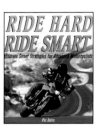